T0335126

WEEKEND MAKES

HOOP EMBROIDERY

25 QUICK AND EASY PROJECTS TO MAKE

WEEKEND MAKES

HOOP EMBROIDERY

25 QUICK AND EASY PROJECTS TO MAKE

ROSEMARY DRYSDALE

First published 2020 by
Guild of Master Craftsman Publications Ltd Castle Place,
166 High Street, Lewes,
East Sussex, BN7 1XU

Text © Rosemary Drysdale, 2020
Copyright in the Work © GMC Publications Ltd, 2020

ISBN 978-1-78494-590-9

All rights reserved.

The right of Rosemary Drysdale to be identified as the
author of this work has been asserted in accordance
with the Copyright, Designs and Patents Act 1988,
sections 77 and 78.

No part of this publication may be reproduced, stored
in a retrieval system or transmitted in any form or by
any means without the prior permission of the publisher
and copyright owner.

This book is sold subject to the condition that all
designs are copyright and are not for commercial
reproduction without the permission of the designer
and copyright owner.

While every effort has been made to obtain permission
from the copyright holders for all material used in this
book, the publishers will be pleased to hear from anyone
who has not been appropriately acknowledged and to
make the correction in future reprints.

The publishers and author can accept no legal
responsibility for any consequences arising from the
application of information, advice or instructions given
in this publication.

A catalogue record for this book is available from the
British Library.

Senior Project Editor: Karin Strom
Managing Art Editor: Darren Brant
Art Editor: Jennifer Stephens
Photography: Quail Studio
Illustrator: Fi Alexandra Hilson

Colour origination by GMC Reprographics
Printed and bound in China

CONTENTS

INTRODUCTION

My love for embroidery began as a young girl growing up in England. Most homes were decorated with embroidered items: pillows, tea towels, tea cosies, tablecloths and bed linens.

Every grandma, mother, aunt and sister had at least one piece of embroidery in progress in her sewing basket.

Embroidery is one of the oldest crafts – its origins can be traced back 30,000 years and it is part of virtually every culture. In recent history, embroidery was popular in Colonial America, Victorian times, and the 1960s. Various exquisite examples of embroidery techniques frequently appear on fashion runways and it is enjoying another renaissance now. It's no wonder embroidery is one of the most relaxing forms of needlework, and with the knowledge of just a few stitches you can create beautiful pieces in just a few hours.

Where do my ideas come from? I just look around! My love of flowers and gardening provide ample inspiration, as you can see in this book. A friend's cat, a colourful bicycle, the birds and the bees can all be fun to stitch

as well. Even a few white snowflakes… the possibilities are endless.

All the projects in this book are framed in the hoops they are worked in, so finishing is a breeze: no framing, sewing or additional materials necessary. Unlike some hobbies, embroidery doesn't require a lot of equipment or a large investment. You probably have some of the tools already. I've provided a list of what you'll need and each pattern has a specific list of everything required to complete it.

I'm so happy to share my love of embroidery with you and hope you will enjoy spending a few weekends relaxing with a hoop, some fabric and beautifully coloured threads, creating an embroidered piece or two for your home or as a gift for a special friend.

You might just get hooked like I did all those years ago!

Rosemary

TOOLS AND MATERIALS

Before starting a project, you'll need to gather some essential items together. If you are a sewer, you probably already have some of the basic tools on hand. The fabrics, threads and embroidery hoops you'll need are readily available at craft and fabric shops, and generally quite affordable.

NEEDLES

Always use a good-quality needle with an eye large enough to allow the thread to slide easily through it. Too small an eye will cause the thread to fray and will be difficult to thread, while too large an eye may leave big holes in the fabric.

- **Embroidery Needles**: They have a fine, sharp point that easily pierces the fabric and come in a variety of sizes ranging from 1 to 10. The higher the number, the finer the needle.

Embroidery needles have a large eye to make threading easier. Do not leave the needle in the work when you are not embroidering as it can leave a mark.

- **Beading Needles**: For the projects using beads, you'll need a beading needle. They have a smaller eye and are very fine so they can fit easily through the bead. Beading needles also come in various sizes. Choose the size you need to fit the beads you are using.

SCISSORS

It's essential to have a high quality pair of embroidery scissors to ensure clean cuts every time.

- A sharp pointed pair of small embroidery scissors with narrow blades.
- A large pair of fabric scissors used only for cutting fabric.

FABRICS

The choice of fabric is key to how your finished project comes out. Always use the best quality fabric available and choose only natural fibres such as linen or cotton. I prefer linen for its lasting qualities and ease of stitching. Most of the pieces in this book are worked on a high-quality, tightly woven linen or a good-quality cotton.

When stretched in the hoop, the fabric should be firm enough to embroider on without puckering or fraying. Avoid loosely woven or nubby fabrics as the design may not transfer completely and the stitches may not lie flat or even. For the projects that include appliquéd felt, like the Colourful Mandala, page 108, choose a high-quality felt. If fabric is called for, as for Vintage Flowers, page 92, choose a tightly woven decorative cotton fabric.

To be sure you have chosen the appropriate fabric, you may want to try a few embroidery stitches on a scrap of the fabric you are going to use to see how they work. Your local craft store may be able to help you choose a fabric if you are unsure.

THREADS

Embroidery threads are available in an array of beautiful colours. For the projects in this book, I've provided colour options in Anchor and DMC thread. I've used either stranded embroidery cotton, also known as floss, or pearl cotton (perle cotton).

Stranded embroidery floss is a divisible thread made up of six individual strands of mercerized cotton that can be separated into single strands, which then can be used as one, two, three or more strands held together to achieve different effects. For most of these projects I used three strands. If different, it's indicated in the pattern instructions.

To separate the strands from the skein, cut an 18in (45cm) length of thread from the skein, hold the thread at the top and pull the threads out one by one upwards to avoid tangling, then place the threads back together side by side before threading into the needle. A longer thread will tangle and knot. You may be tempted to use a longer thread, but 18in (45cm) is perfect.

Pearl cotton is a non-divisible embroidery cotton with a tight twist and a beautiful sheen. It comes in skeins or balls and is only used as a single thread. There are three different sizes available: size 3, 5 or 8. Size 3 is the thickest.

Note: Each skein or ball of thread has its own colour number and I have listed the colour numbers used for each project. If the suggested thread colour is not available, choose a shade as close as possible to my recommended choice.

HOOPS

Embroidery hoops come in a wide range of sizes, shapes and materials. They keep the fabric taut and flat as you are working on it, so you can keep your stitches even. In this book, we are also using them as frames to display the finished pieces.

A hoop consists of two removable rings held firmly together by a metal screw, which is used to tighten the hoop when the fabric is in place.

I use wooden hoops for my embroideries, but you can find them in metal and various shades of plastic. They come in sizes from small to large, and round, oval, square or rectangle shapes. Round hoops are the most popular and are what I've chosen for the projects in this book.

BEADS AND BUTTONS

Some of the embroideries in the book use beads and others use buttons. You can use buttons you have to hand or purchase new ones. I've indicated what sizes I used, but play around with colours, sizes and shapes to customize your design.

For the projects using seed beads, I recommend the size indicated in the pattern. You can purchase seed beads in packets and the appropriate bead needle size will be indicated on the packet.

YOU WILL ALSO NEED
- Ruler or tape measure
- Ironing board and iron
- Sewing thread for basting
- Pencil
- Water-soluble pen
- Dressmaker's carbon paper
- Tracing paper
- Masking tape

EMBROIDERY BASICS

Whether you are brand new to embroidery or have some experience, these key steps will help you create display-ready projects to gift or keep.

GETTING STARTED

HOW TO TRANSFER A DESIGN

To transfer the drawing onto the fabric, you will need a firm surface to work on such as a board or table.

1. First trace the line drawing from the page onto the tracing paper. Lie the fabric (A) onto the hard surface and tape flat.

2. Next put the carbon paper, coloured side down (B), over the fabric, centring the traced design (C) on top. Tape it down to secure. Using the pencil, trace around the line drawing, pressing hard. Check at a corner to make sure the design is transferring onto the fabric.

Note: If you prefer a different method, you can use a lightbox or bright window and a water-soluble marking pen. First you would tape the tracing paper with the line drawing onto the lightbox or window. Then tape down the fabric over the tracing paper and use the pen to trace the design onto the fabric. When the stitching is completed, immerse the embroidery in cold water and the water-soluble ink will wash away. Never use hot water or an iron as it will set the ink.

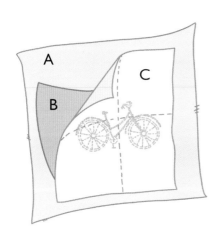

PUTTING THE FABRIC IN THE HOOP WITHOUT A LINING

After transferring the design onto the fabric, you are ready to place it into the hoop.

1. First loosen the metal screw on the hoop. You will now have two rings: a smaller inner ring and a slightly larger outer ring. Place the inner ring under the fabric, centring the design. The drawing will be facing you.

1

2. Push the outer ring over the inner ring, keeping the screw at the top of the hoop. Tighten the screw, pulling the edges of the fabric a little to get the fabric taut. When the design is centred, you are ready to stitch.

2

PUTTING THE FABRIC IN THE HOOP WITH A LINING

A lining is a second piece of fabric placed in the hoop along with the embroidery fabric. I like to use felt, but a cotton fabric would also be suitable. Most of the projects in this book didn't require a lining, but it can helpful when the embroidery fabric of your choice is a little sheer and the edges of the hoop and the stitches on the wrong side of the embroidery shadow through. I also use a lining when certain stitches are worked without starting and stopping the threads, so a line of thread forms on the wrong side and shows through. A good example of this is the French knots on the Cat in the Window on page 30.

Both the fabric and the lining are in the hoop, with the lining facing you. Trim the extra lining close to the edge of the inner hoop, taking care not to cut the embroidery fabric.

FINISHING

When you're done stitching your piece, take the time to finish it neatly so it's beautiful on both sides. I've done what is called a gathered finish.

1. With a long length of pearl cotton and the wrong side facing, insert the needle into the fabric about ½in (13mm) from the outer edge of the hoop. Work a circle of running stitches around the perimeter of the hoop. Leave a long tail.

1

2. Using embroidery scissors, trim off excess fabric at least ½in (13mm) away from the running stitches. Gather the running stitches by pulling the pearl cotton thread until the fabric fits snugly around the inner hoop, then secure the thread with a few double stitches.

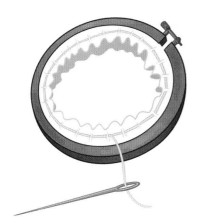

2

3. Place the felt backing on top of the fabric and, using pearl cotton, stitch through both the felt and fabric to attach the backing.

3

EMBROIDERY STITCHES

STARTING A STITCH

To begin a stitch we use an "away knot" on the front of the work. (An away knot is worked 3–5in (7.6–12.7cm) away from the area where the embroidery begins.) Tie a knot at the end of the thread you are working with and take the needle down through the front of the fabric to the back, about 3–5in (7.6–12.7cm) "away" from where your first stitch is to begin. A long thread will be secured on the back of the work. After the stitch is completed, cut off the knot from the front of the work and thread the long thread onto the needle and weave it securely under the stitches on the back of the embroidery.

ENDING A STITCH

Take the thread to the wrong side of your work and weave it under the worked stitches for about 2in (5cm). Try to keep the wrong side of your work as neat as possible.

STRAIGHT STITCH

One of the most basic stitches, it can be worked long or short, evenly or different lengths.

Bring needle up through at A and down at B. Pull tightly enough that there is no gap, but not so tight that the fabric puckers.

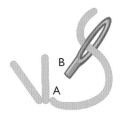

RUNNING STITCH

If you know how to hand sew at all, you know how to do a running stitch!

Working from right to left, bring the needle up at A, go in at B and come back out at C. Continue in this manner, spacing stitches evenly. To end the stitch, go down through the fabric to the wrong side at B.

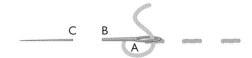

BACK STITCH

This utilitarian stitch can be used for outlines, or anywhere you need to "draw" with thread.

Working from right to left, bring the needle up at A and make a small backwards stitch by going down at B. Bring the needle through at C. Move the needle to the left under the fabric. Continue this pattern, bringing the needle up a space ahead and down into the hole made by the last stitch. To end the stitch, go down through the fabric to the wrong side at C.

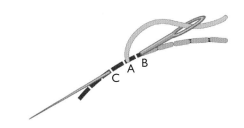

CROSS STITCH

Two stitches that cross each other to form an X, cross stitch can be worked individually or in rows.

1. Working from left to right, bring needle up at A and down at B. If you are working a row of cross stitches, continue working slanted stitches evenly in this manner.

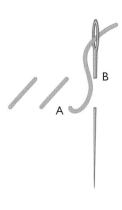

2. On the return, work from right to left, crossing over the first stitches from C to D, forming a cross. To end the stitch, go down through the fabric to the wrong side at D.

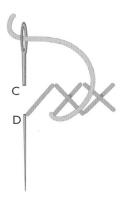

STEM STITCH

Stem stitch is most often used to make straight or curved lines, or as a filling stitch. The thread can be held to the left of needle, as shown, or to the right. Use shorter stitches when working curved lines.

1. Bring the needle up at A, in at B and back up again at C. Draw the thread through and hold to the left of the needle.

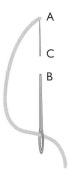

2. Bring the needle in at D and up again through B.

3. Continue Step 2, always holding the thread to the left of the needle. To end the stitch, go down through the fabric to wrong side at D.

CHAIN STITCH

Chain stitch is one of the most versatile stitches. It's basically a series, or chain, of loops. It can be used as an outline or filler. Single chain stitches are often used individually or to make flower petals, called lazy daisy. Zigzag chain stitch uses chain stitches worked at an angle to create a zigzag effect.

I. Bring needle through fabric at A. Form a loop and hold down with your thumb or finger. Insert needle at A again and come back through fabric at B. Gently pull thread through to form first chain.

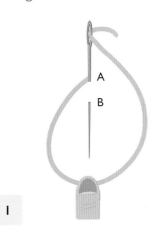

2. Repeat Step 1, always inserting needle where thread came out, drawing it through tightly enough to lay flat, but not so tight that the fabric puckers.

SINGLE CHAIN STITCH

Follow step 1 for chain stitch. Go down through fabric at C, tacking the top of the stitch down. To end stitch, go down to wrong side of fabric at C. Fasten off.

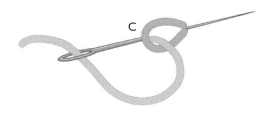

LAZY DAISY

Follow instructions for single chain. Bring the needle back through the fabric next to the base of the first petal to form the next petal.

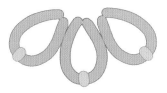

ZIGZAG CHAIN STITCH

Work exactly like chain stitch, but inserting the needle at an angle, rather than vertical.

FRENCH KNOT

A favourite stitch of embroiderers, the French knot can be used as an individual element, like an eye, scattered about randomly, or used to fill in an entire area to create texture. The basic French knot is wrapped once, but you can wrap it twice, three or even four times to create a larger knot.

1. Bring needle up at A and twist through the thread bring it over the needle.

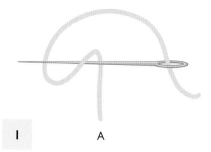

1   A

2. Pull the needle up over the thread and back down into A.

2   A

3. You are essentially tying a knot with the needle and thread. For a French knot wrapped twice, twist the thread over the needle twice in Step 1.

3

BLANKET STITCH

This is a fun and versatile stitch that instantly adds a finished, vintage look to a piece. Stitches can be made close together for a solid look or spaced out for a more open effect.

1. Bring the thread up at A. Insert the needle in at B and back out at C, holding the thread under the needle. Draw through.

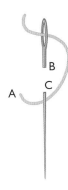

2. Repeat Step 1, spacing the stitches evenly.

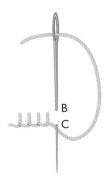

3. To end the stitch, go down through fabric to wrong side at C. To work a curved or round shape, work stitches evenly around the edge, opening up the space between stitches.

FLY STITCH

This Y-shaped stitch works well for leaves and foliage.

1. Bring needle up at A and insert needle at B, to the right of A. Pull needle out at C, bringing the tip of the needle over the thread.

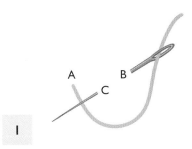

2. Pull the needle through the fabric, looping it over the stitch, pulling it down at D to form a Y-shape.

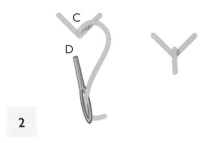

3. Continue in this way to form a neat vertical row.

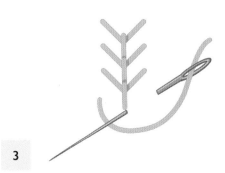

HERRINGBONE STITCH

Herringbone makes a great border and can be worked on a large scale or small. You are making diagonal stitches that cross each other.

1. Bring needle up at A and down at B, at a diagonal from A.

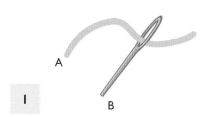

2. Bring needle up at C, level with B. Then bring needle down at D, level with A.

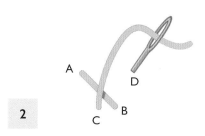

3. Bring needle up at E, slightly to the left of and level with D. Then bring down at F.

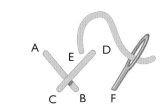

4. Continue, making a herringbone pattern. To end the stitch, go down through the fabric to wrong side at F.

SPLIT STITCH

Often used for outlines to be filled with other stitches, the split stitch can also be worked in rows together.

1. Bring the needle up at A and down at B.

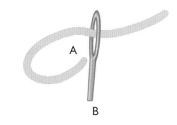

2. Bring the needle up at C, through the centre of the thread, splitting the stitch in half.

3. Continue by bringing needle through at D. To end the stitch, go down through the fabric to wrong side at D.

SATIN STITCH

Satin stitch is a wonderful way to fill in small shapes. For neater edges, try outlining the area with split stitch. Working at a slight angle is much easier than straight across or up and down. For more dimension, you can use a padded satin stitch, where you can work the base row straight.

1. Outline the area you want to fill.

2. Beginning at the centre of the area you want to fill in, bring the needle up through the front of the fabric from A and down through B.

3. Bring the needle up through C, staying as close to the first stitch as possible.

4. Continue with this stitch until the area is filled. To end the stitch, go down through fabric to the wrong side at B.

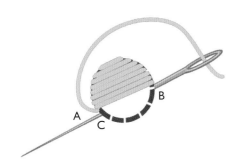

OUTLINED SATIN STITCH

1. Outline the shape in split stitch.

2. Work satin stitches over the split stitch outline to form a neat edge.

COUCHING STITCH

Couching is a way to tack down one thread by using small stitches with another thread.

Place the main thread along a marked line. With either a matching thread or contrasting colour thread, bring the needle up just below main thread at A and insert just above it at B, securing the long thread with small stitches. To end the stitch, go down through the fabric to the wrong side at B.

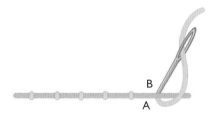

LONG AND SHORT STITCH

Also known as tapestry shading, this stitch can be used to fill in larger areas. You can create subtle shading by blending colours, from light to dark or dark to light. It's almost like painting with thread.

1. Work a row of split stitch along the outline. This will help you maintain a neat edge. Bring your needle up through the fabric at A and back down at B, going just over the outline stitch. Work one long stitch and one short stitch right next to each other. (Make the short stitch about three-quarters of the length of the long stitch.

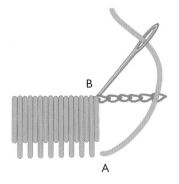

2. For the next row, using another shade of thread, work all stitches the same length from C to D, but stagger them. (All of the stitches should be the same length, but you are inserting them into long and short stitches of the previous row, so creating a staggered effect.)

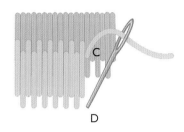

3. Using a third shade of thread, work another row of stitches in the same manner, from E to F.

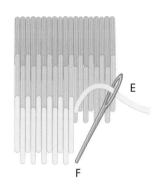

SHAPED LONG AND SHORT STITCH

This is worked the same as long and short stitch, however you can create any shape by following the diagram.

1. Work a row of split stitch around the outline of your shape. Come up at A, go down at B, making a long stitch. Then go up at C and next to B, making a long stitch.

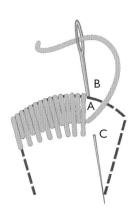

2. For the next row, using another shade of thread, work all long stitches, staggering them. Continue until you have finished filling the outline, changing the shade of thread for each new row.

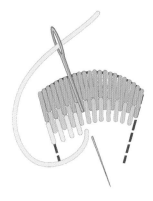

FISHBONE STITCH

Fishbone can be worked placing stitches right next to each other or spaced out for a more open look. It's worked off a centre line.

1. Bring needle up at A, at the centre point of the shape, and down at B, below it on the centre line. Bring thread up at C, just to the left of A following the outline of your shape.

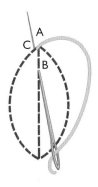

2. Bring needle down at D, keeping the thread under the needle, forming a loop and drawing through.

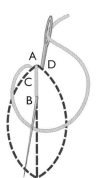

3. Bring needle down at E, right below B, and come up at F.

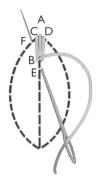

4. Continue forming loops and tying down with small, straight stitches. To end, go down through the fabric to wrong side at E.

5. Finished fishbone effect.

BLACK AND WHITE

Graphic one-colour stitching makes for a great first embroidery project and this is an excellent way to learn the most basic stitches. Use black thread, as I've done here, to create a modern graphic look for this botanical trio, or choose red or navy thread for a more traditional effect.

SKILL LEVEL: EASY

FOR EACH DESIGN, YOU'LL NEED

FABRIC

- 9in (23cm) square white linen fabric

- 4¾in (12cm) circle white felt, for backing

HOOP

- 5in (12.7cm) embroidery hoop

HABERDASHERY

- Thread: pearl cotton 8
  Black (Anchor 403, DMC 310)

- Thread for finishing: pearl cotton 5,
  White (Anchor 001, DMC White)

- Embroidery needle, size 6

- Dressmaker's carbon paper and tracing paper

- Pencil

- Scissors

> **Tip**
>
> Play with the positive-negative effect by using the dark colour for the background and embroidering with white thread.

FOR DAISY
PREPARATION

Transfer the design (see Templates, page 140) onto the fabric (see page 11). Centre hoop over the design, assembling it securely (see page 12).

STITCHES USED
SEE EMBROIDERY STITCHES, PAGES 14-23

- French knot
- Stem stitch
- Single chain stitch

METHOD

Using one strand of pearl cotton throughout, work the embroidery following the stitch diagrams carefully.

FINISHING

See instructions for gathered finish and attaching a felt backing on page 13.

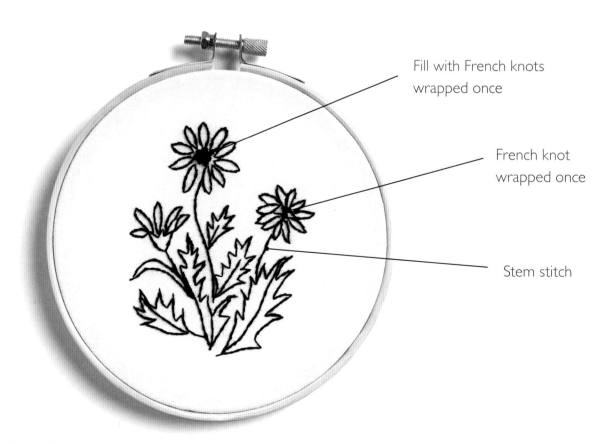

Fill with French knots wrapped once

French knot wrapped once

Stem stitch

FOR DANDELION PREPARATION

Transfer the design (see Templates, page 140) onto fabric (see page 11). Centre hoop over the design, assembling it securely (see page 12).

STITCHES USED
SEE EMBROIDERY STITCHES, PAGES 14-23

- Single chain stitch
- Straight stitch
- Back stitch
- French knot
- Stem stitch

METHOD

Using one strand of pearl cotton throughout, work the embroidery following the stitch diagrams carefully.

FINISHING

See instructions for gathered finish and attaching a felt backing on page 13.

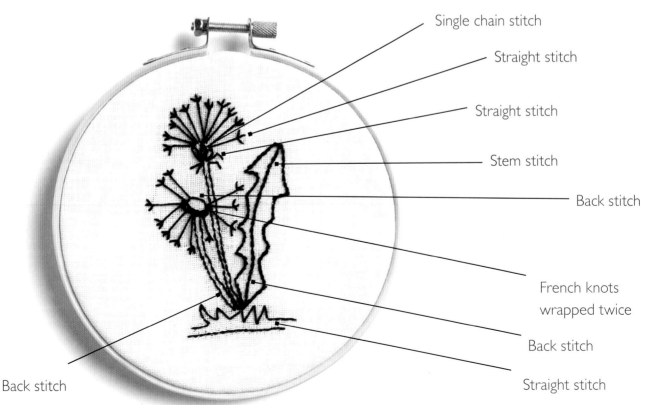

Single chain stitch

Straight stitch

Straight stitch

Stem stitch

Back stitch

French knots wrapped twice

Back stitch

Straight stitch

Back stitch

FOR WINTER TREE PREPARATION

....

Transfer the design (see Templates, page 140) onto fabric (see page 11). Centre hoop over the design, assembling it securely (see page 12).

STITCHES USED
SEE EMBROIDERY STITCHES, PAGES 14-23

- Lazy daisy

- Straight stitch

- Back stitch

- French knot

- Running stitch

METHOD
Using one strand of pearl cotton throughout, work the embroidery following the stitch diagrams.

FINISHING
See instructions for gathered finish and attaching a felt backing on page 13.

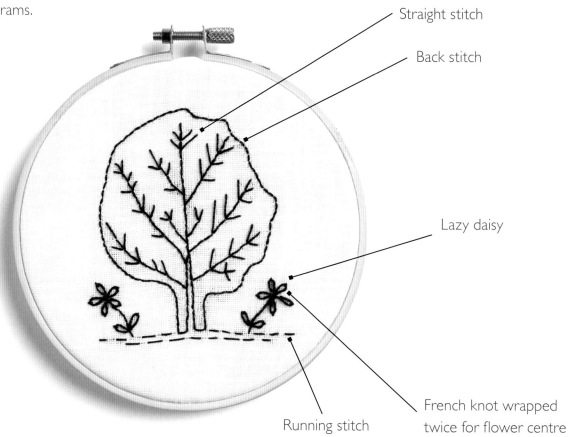

Straight stitch

Back stitch

Lazy daisy

French knot wrapped twice for flower centre

Running stitch

CAT IN THE WINDOW

Who doesn't love cute cats? This classic cat in the window would make a great gift for a cat-loving friend. You could always change the colour to resemble their feline friend.

SKILL LEVEL: EASY

YOU'LL NEED

FABRIC
- 9in (23cm) square white linen fabric
- 9in (23cm) square white felt, for lining
- 4¾in (12cm) circle white felt, for backing

HOOP
- 5in (12.7cm) embroidery hoop

HABERDASHERY
- Thread: embroidery floss
    Black (Anchor 403, DMC 310)
    Blue (Anchor 131, DMC 798)
    Light Brown (Anchor 347, DMC 3064)
- Thread for finishing: pearl cotton 5, White (Anchor 001, DMC White)
- Embroidery needle, size 6
- Dressmaker's carbon paper and tracing paper
- Pencil
- Scissors

PREPARATION

Transfer the design (see Templates, page 130) onto fabric (see page 11). Centre hoop over the design, assembling it securely (see page 12).

STITCHES USED
SEE EMBROIDERY STITCHES, PAGES 14-23

- Satin stitch

- Back stitch

- Straight stitch

- Stem stitch

- French knot

METHOD

Work the embroidery following the diagram for strands and stitches, except for the French knots, which you work last. Remove the embroidered piece from the hoop and centre the lining felt on top of the wrong side of the embroidery and centre back in the hoop. (You now have two layers of fabric.) Using six strands of floss, work the French knots through both the felt lining and the linen fabric.

FINISHING

See instructions for gathered finish and attaching a felt backing on page 13.

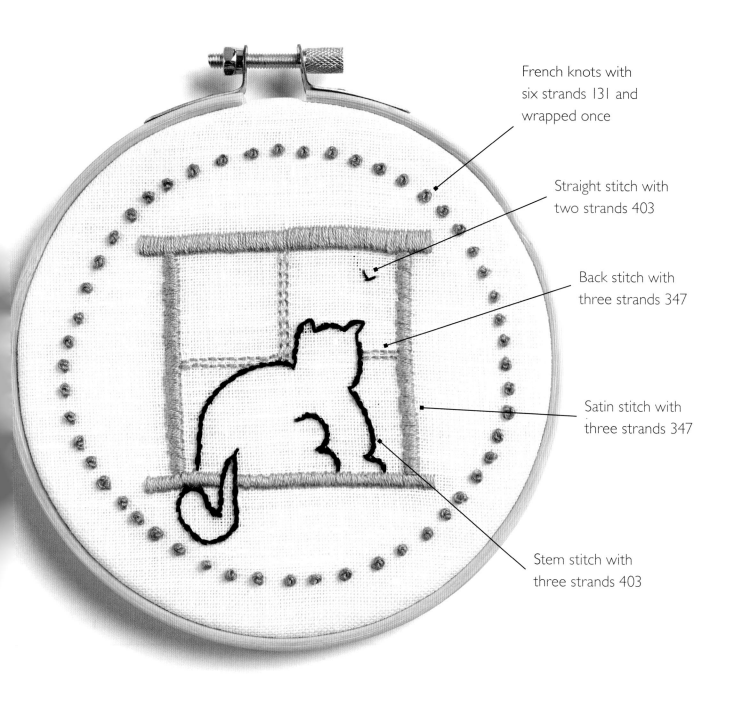

French knots with
six strands 131 and
wrapped once

Straight stitch with
two strands 403

Back stitch with
three strands 347

Satin stitch with
three strands 347

Stem stitch with
three strands 403

SEASHELLS

Since I live by the sea, beach walks and shell gathering are frequent activities with my family. I love the simple yet complex nature of the shells I collect. Stitch a few of my favourites for your own summerhouse or to give as a gift when you go visiting.

SKILL LEVEL: EASY

YOU'LL NEED

FABRIC

- 9in (23cm) square ecru linen fabric

- 4¾in (12cm) circle white felt, for backing

HOOP

- 5in (12.7cm) embroidery hoop

HABERDASHERY

- Thread: embroidery floss
      White (Anchor 002, DMC White)
      Light Brown (Anchor 376, DMC 3776)
      Dark Brown (Anchor 337, DMC 842)

- Thread for finishing: pearl cotton 5,
  White (Anchor 001, DMC White)

- Embroidery needle, size 6

- Dressmaker's carbon paper and tracing paper

- Pencil

- Scissors

Tips

You really only need to know two simple stitches to make these detailed shells. I was able to create fairly complex shell "drawings" by placing lots of rows of back stitches fairly close together.

When choosing your fabric for this project, look for a natural linen or something with a sandy look.

PREPARATION

Transfer the design (see Templates, page 130) onto fabric (see page 11). Centre hoop over the design, assembling it securely (see page 12).

STITCHES USED

SEE EMBROIDERY STITCHES, PAGES 14-23

- Back stitch

- French knot

METHOD

Using three strands of floss throughout, work the embroidery following the diagram. Work the back stitches first, then the French knots.

FINISHING

See instructions for gathered finish and attaching a felt backing on page 13.

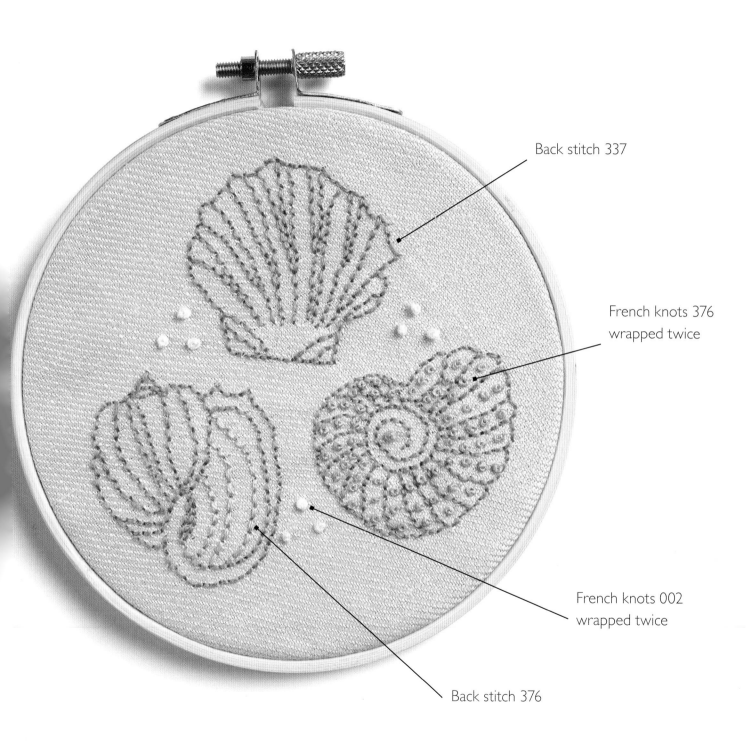

Back stitch 337

French knots 376
wrapped twice

French knots 002
wrapped twice

Back stitch 376

HANGING BASKETS

Get into the houseplant trend even if you don't have green fingers. Whether you choose to make just one or both – you'll practise your stitches and learn how to make a simple tassel. And you don't even need to know how to macramé!

SKILL LEVEL: REQUIRES SOME EXPERIENCE

FOR EACH DESIGN, YOU'LL NEED

FABRIC
- 9in (23cm) square white linen fabric
- 4¾in (12cm) circle white felt, for backing

HOOP
- 5in (12.7cm) embroidery hoop

HABERDASHERY
- Thread: see individual patterns
- Thread for finishing: pearl cotton 5, White (Anchor 001, DMC White)
- Embroidery needle, size 6
- Dressmaker's carbon paper and tracing paper
- Pencil
- Scissors

> ### Tip
>
> According to one of the basic principles of interior design, things are more visually pleasing when grouped in odd numbers. If you do decide to make more than two planters, vary the position of the green threads and try displaying them clustered in a group.

FOR FERN:
- Thread: embroidery floss
    Dark Green (Anchor 258, DMC 904)
    Light Green (Anchor 240, DMC 164)
    Dark Brown (Anchor 359, DMC 801)
    Light Brown (Anchor 347, DMC 3064)

FOR LEAVES:
- Thread: pearl cotton 8
    Light Brown (Anchor 366, DMC 951)
    Dark Brown (Anchor 358, DMC 433)
    Light Green (Anchor 238, DMC 703)
    Dark Green (Anchor 229, DMC 910)

FOR FERN
PREPARATION

Transfer the design (see Templates, page 136) onto fabric (see page 11). Centre hoop over the design, assembling it securely (see page 12).

STITCHES USED
SEE EMBROIDERY STITCHES, PAGES 14-23

- Straight stitch

- Stem stitch

- Satin stitch

METHOD

Work the embroidery following the diagram for strands and stitches. Work the pot first, then most of the fern fronds, referring to the photo. Next, work the basket cords using six strands of floss. Work the four fronds that go over the basket cords, referring to the diagram. Next, work the basket cords using six strands of floss, working one long stitch from the top where the threads meet, to the top of the pot. Then make another stitch from the top of the pot to the bottom where the threads meet again. Make an eight-strand tassel (see diagram), and sew onto the fabric where the basket cords meet at the bottom of the pot, referring to the photo for placement.

FINISHING

See instructions for gathered finish and attaching a felt backing on page 13.

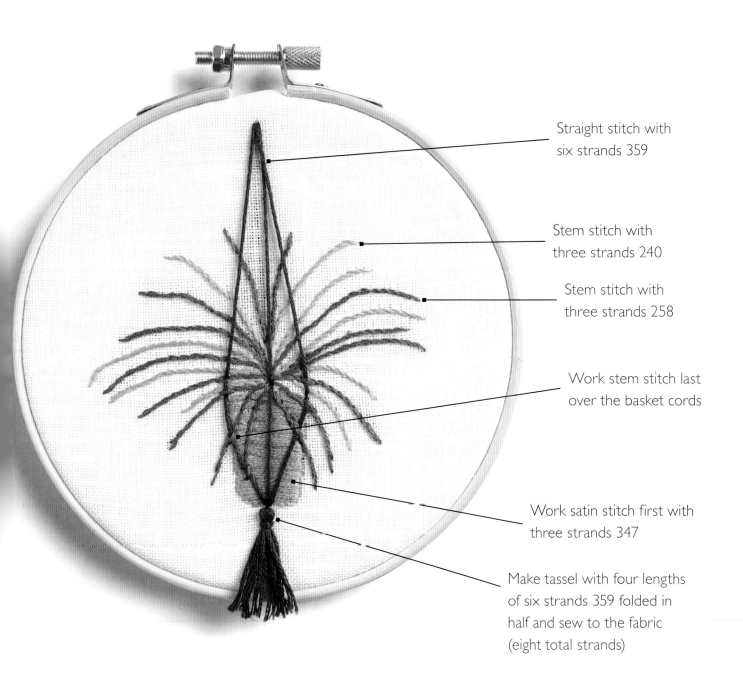

Straight stitch with
six strands 359

Stem stitch with
three strands 240

Stem stitch with
three strands 258

Work stem stitch last
over the basket cords

Work satin stitch first with
three strands 347

Make tassel with four lengths
of six strands 359 folded in
half and sew to the fabric
(eight total strands)

FOR LEAVES
PREPARATION

Transfer the design (see Templates, page 136) onto fabric (see page 11). Centre hoop over the design, assembling it securely (see page 12).

STITCHES USED
SEE EMBROIDERY STITCHES, PAGES 14-23

- Straight stitch

- Chain stitch

- Stem stitch

- Satin stitch

- Back stitch

METHOD

Using pearl cotton throughout, work the embroidery following the diagrams. Work the pot first, then the foliage, then the cord, using one long stitch for each strand of the cord. Make an eight-strand tassel (see diagram), and sew onto the fabric at the centre bottom of the pot, referring to the photo for placement.

FINISHING

See instructions for gathered finish and attaching a felt backing on page 13.

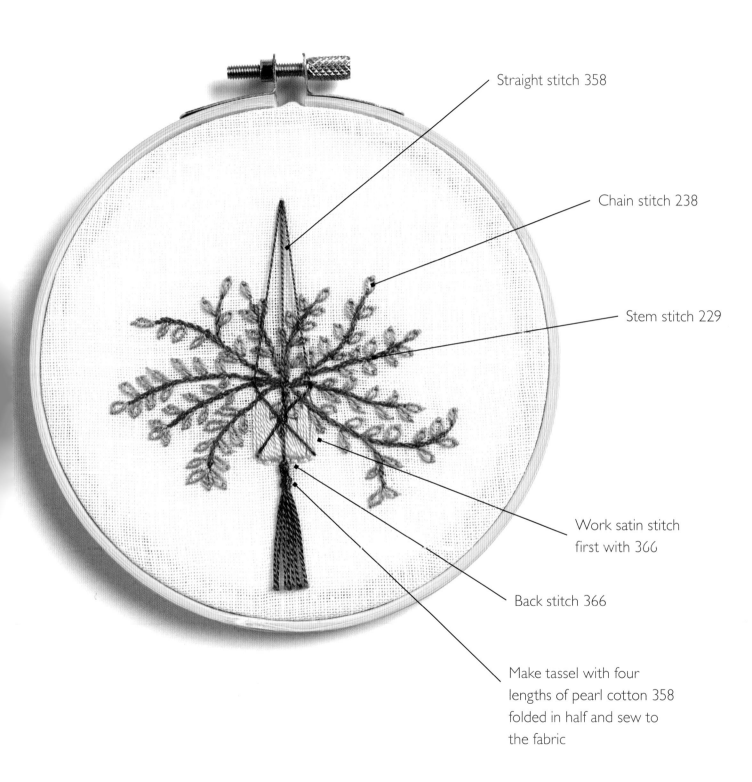

Straight stitch 358

Chain stitch 238

Stem stitch 229

Work satin stitch first with 366

Back stitch 366

Make tassel with four lengths of pearl cotton 358 folded in half and sew to the fabric

FANTASY FLORALS

I get a lot of inspiration from nature, especially flowers. Floral motifs mix well with almost every decor and can be stylized accordingly. Practise your French knots, fishbone stitch and running stitches to create flowers that are full of personality with an updated look.

SKILL LEVEL: REQUIRES SOME EXPERIENCE

YOU'LL NEED

FABRIC

- 12in (30cm) square white linen fabric

- 7¾in (19cm) circle white felt, for backing

HOOP

- 8in (20.3cm) embroidery hoop

HABERDASHERY

- Thread: pearl cotton 8
    Dark Green (Anchor 268, DMC 937)
    Medium Green (Anchor 266, DMC 471)
    Light Green (Anchor 213, DMC 504)
    Light Acid Green (Anchor 264, DMC 3348)
    Light Blue (Anchor 167, DMC 3766)
    Medium Blue (Anchor 146, DMC 798)
    Dark Blue (Anchor 133, DMC 796)
    Light Lilac (Anchor 108, DMC 210)
    Medium Lilac (Anchor 110, DMC 333)
    Dark Lilac (Anchor 101, DMC 550)

- Thread for finishing: pearl cotton 5, White (Anchor 001, DMC White)

- Embroidery needle, size 6

- Dressmaker's carbon paper and tracing paper

- Pencil

- Scissors

> **Tip**
>
> With many of the projects in this book you can change the look by varying the background colour or shades of thread. Try to think out of the box! Bright flowers really pop off a dark background for example. Or, take some cues from nature and try toned-down colours for an autumnal look.

PREPARATION

Transfer the design (see Templates, page 137) onto fabric (see page 11). Centre hoop over the design, assembling it securely (see page 12).

STITCHES USED
SEE EMBROIDERY STITCHES, PAGES 14-23

- French knot

- Chain stitch

- Single chain stitch

- Running stitch

- Stem stitch

- Back stitch

- Fishbone stitch

METHOD
Work the stems first, then the flowers, adding the French knots last.

FINISHING
See instructions for gathered finish and attaching a felt backing on page 13.

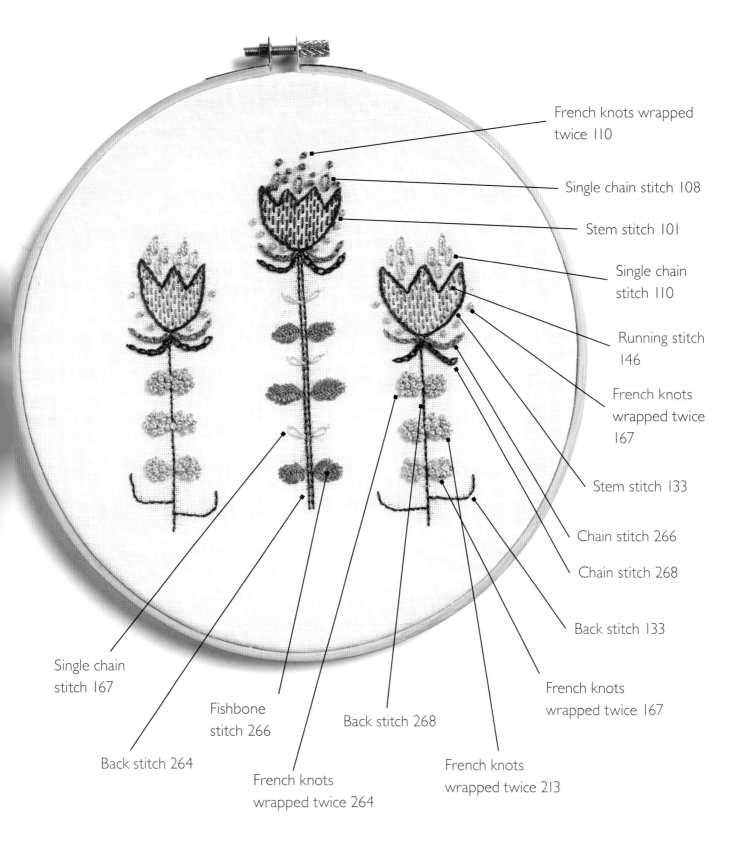

French knots wrapped twice 110

Single chain stitch 108

Stem stitch 101

Single chain stitch 110

Running stitch 146

French knots wrapped twice 167

Stem stitch 133

Chain stitch 266

Chain stitch 268

Back stitch 133

French knots wrapped twice 167

Single chain stitch 167

Fishbone stitch 266

Back stitch 268

French knots wrapped twice 213

Back stitch 264

French knots wrapped twice 264

BERRY WREATH

The easiest way to create dimension is with one of my favourite and most versatile stitches, the French knot. To get knots that really pop, I simply wrap them several times – these berries are all wrapped four times.

SKILL LEVEL: EASY

YOU'LL NEED

FABRIC
- 7½in (19cm) square white linen fabric
- 2¾in (6cm) square white felt, for backing

HOOP
- 3in (7.6cm) embroidery hoop

HABERDASHERY
- Thread: pearl cotton 8
    Purple (Anchor 101, DMC 550)
    Blue (Anchor 148, DMC 311)
    Green (Anchor 226, DMC 702)

- Thread for finishing: pearl cotton 5,
  White (Anchor 001, DMC White)

- Embroidery needle, size 6

- Dressmaker's carbon paper and tracing paper

- Pencil

- Scissors

Tip

I chose purple and blue for my wreath to resemble berries, but you could use any colour combos you like. Orange and yellow or pink and blue or two shades of green. Better yet, do them all and create a little collection!

PREPARATION

Transfer the design (see Templates, page 131) onto fabric (see page 11). Centre hoop over the design, assembling it securely (see page 12).

STITCHES USED

SEE EMBROIDERY STITCHES, PAGES 14-23

- Single chain stitch

- French knot

- Straight stitch

METHOD

First fill the circles with French knots, then work the leaves.

FINISHING

See instructions for gathered finish and attaching a felt backing on page 13.

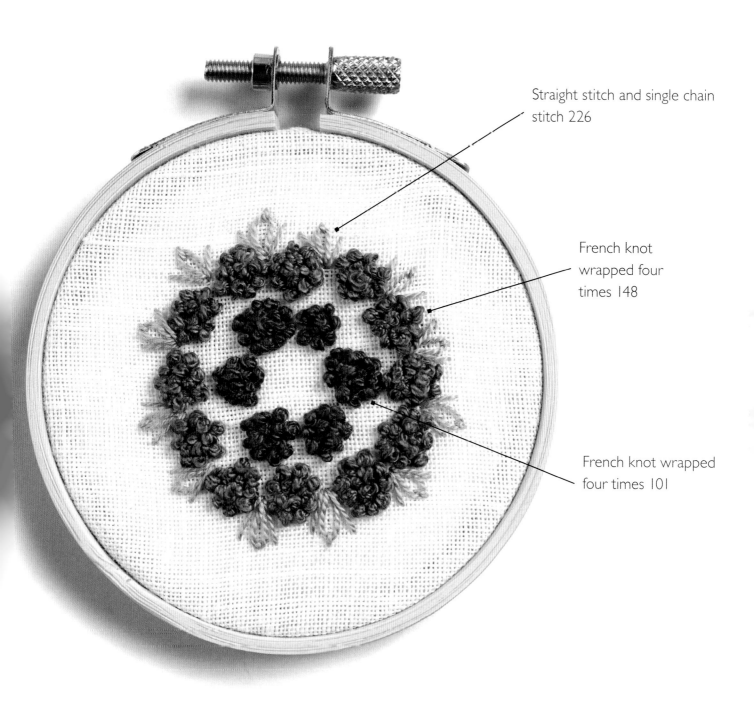

Straight stitch and single chain stitch 226

French knot wrapped four times 148

French knot wrapped four times 101

MEADOW CLOVER

You can make realistic-looking clover blossoms by using three strands of embroidery floss held together and chain-stitching so closely that the stitches overlap each other. Subtle shading done with two closely related tones of floss adds to the lifelike look. It's like drawing with thread!

SKILL LEVEL: REQUIRES SOME EXPERIENCE

YOU'LL NEED

FABRIC
- 10in (25cm) square white linen fabric
- 5¾in (15cm) square white felt, for backing

HOOP
- 6in (16.2cm) embroidery hoop

HABERDASHERY
- Thread: embroidery floss
    Light Green (Anchor 259, DMC 772)
    Dark Green (Anchor 875, DMC 3817)
    Light Purple (Anchor 95, DMC 3609)
    Dark Purple (Anchor 96, DMC 3608)

- Thread for finishing: pearl cotton 5, White (Anchor 001, DMC White)

- Embroidery needle, size 6

- Dressmaker's carbon paper and tracing paper

- Pencil

- Scissors

> **Tip**
>
> When stitching the blossoms, start at the top and work down, so you're working from light to dark. Then add the sepal (the green section that connects the flower to the stem).

PREPARATION

. . . .

Transfer the design (see Templates, page 139)
onto fabric (see page 11). Centre hoop over
the design, assembling it securely (see page 12).

STITCHES USED
SEE EMBROIDERY STITCHES, PAGES 14-23

- Single chain stitch

- Fishbone stitch

- Satin stitch

- Stem stitch

METHOD
Work the stems first, then the leaves. Work
the clover blossoms last.

FINISHING
See instructions for gathered finish and
attaching a felt backing on page 13.

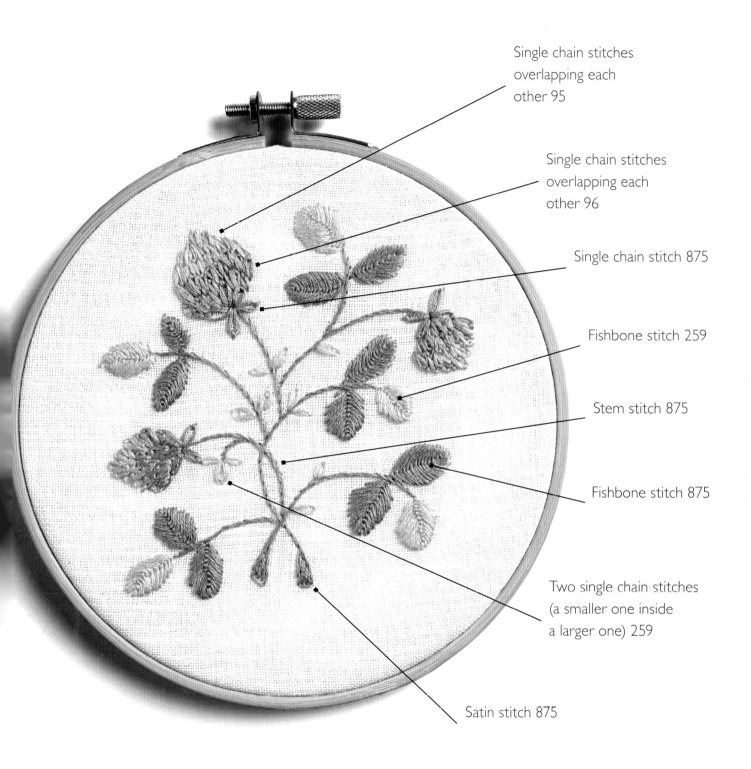

Single chain stitches overlapping each other 95

Single chain stitches overlapping each other 96

Single chain stitch 875

Fishbone stitch 259

Stem stitch 875

Fishbone stitch 875

Two single chain stitches (a smaller one inside a larger one) 259

Satin stitch 875

BICYCLE & BALLOONS

*Balloons, wheels and gears: you'll get lots of practice making circles on this fun turquoise bike.
Add a basket of flowers and off you go!*

SKILL LEVEL: REQUIRES SOME EXPERIENCE

YOU'LL NEED

FABRIC

- 12in (30cm) square white linen fabric

- 7¾in (19cm) circle white felt, for backing

HOOP

- 8in (20cm) embroidery hoop

HABERDASHERY

- Thread: embroidery floss
    Red (Anchor 46, DMC 666)
    Orange (Anchor 324, DMC 721)
    Light Grey (Anchor 234, DMC 762)
    Dark Grey (Anchor 236, DMC 413)
    Yellow (Anchor 290, DMC 444)
    Light Yellow (Anchor 292, DMC 3078)
    Green (Anchor 258, DMC 904)
    Turquoise (Anchor 187, DMC 958)
    Light Brown (Anchor 347, DMC 3064)
    Black (Anchor 403, DMC 310)

- Thread for finishing: pearl cotton 5,
  White (Anchor 001, DMC White)

- Embroidery needle, size 6

- Dressmaker's carbon paper and tracing paper

- Pencil

- Scissors

Tips

For the bicycle frame use one strand of turquoise floss to make an outline with split stitch and then fill in with satin stitch. This will make a neater edge.

Work the basket before the flowers and leaves.

PREPARATION

Transfer the design (see Templates, page 128) onto fabric (see page 11). Centre hoop over the design, assembling it securely (see page 12).

STITCHES USED
SEE EMBROIDERY STITCHES, PAGES 14-23

- Stem stitch

- Satin stitch

- Outlined satin stitch

- Chain stitch

- Lazy daisy

- French knot

- Back stitch

- Straight stitch

METHOD

Work the bicycle wheels and gears first, then the frame. Next work the balloons, then the basket, working the flowers and foliage last.

FINISHING

See instructions for gathered finish and attaching a felt backing on page 13.

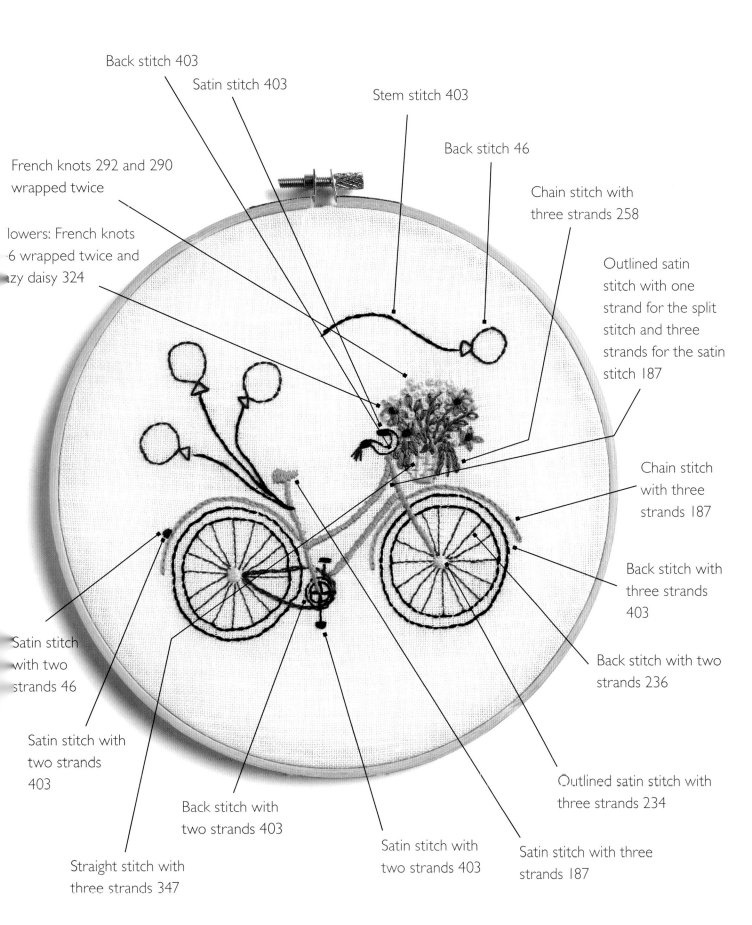

Back stitch 403

Satin stitch 403

Stem stitch 403

Back stitch 46

Chain stitch with three strands 258

French knots 292 and 290 wrapped twice

Outlined satin stitch with one strand for the split stitch and three strands for the satin stitch 187

lowers: French knots 6 wrapped twice and azy daisy 324

Chain stitch with three strands 187

Satin stitch with two strands 46

Back stitch with three strands 403

Satin stitch with two strands 403

Back stitch with two strands 236

Back stitch with two strands 403

Outlined satin stitch with three strands 234

Straight stitch with three strands 347

Satin stitch with two strands 403

Satin stitch with three strands 187

WHIMSICAL DAISIES

Clusters of French knots form the centres of these dancing daisies. I've chosen a traditional yellow and white variety for inspiration, but you could make a sunflower version with brown centres and yellow petals.

SKILL LEVEL: EASY

YOU'LL NEED

FABRIC
- 10in (25cm) square grey linen fabric
- 5¾in (15cm) circle white felt, for backing

HOOP
- 6in (15.25cm) embroidery hoop

HABERDASHERY
- Thread: embroidery floss
  White (Anchor 002, DMC White)
  Yellow (Anchor 301, DMC 744)
  Light Green (Anchor 875, DMC 3817)
  Dark Green (Anchor 212, DMC 561)

- Thread for finishing: pearl cotton 5,
  White (Anchor 001, DMC White)

- Embroidery needle, size 6

- Dressmaker's carbon paper and tracing paper

- Pencil

- Scissors

Tip

Another way to change up the look of your project is to vary the background colour. Use a darker fabric for a more dramatic look or stay with light tones for a softer effect. Experiment by holding the embroidery threads against the fabric before you begin stitching to be sure there is enough contrast.

PREPARATION

Transfer the design (see Templates, page 139) onto fabric (see page 11). Centre hoop over the design, assembling it securely (see page 12).

STITCHES USED
SEE EMBROIDERY STITCHES, PAGES 14-23

- French knot

- Single chain stitch

- Satin stitch

- Stem stitch

METHOD

Using three strands of embroidery floss throughout, work the embroidery following the diagram. First work the stems, then the leaves, then the petals. Add the French knots. Work the circle of petals around the design last.

FINISHING

See instructions for gathered finish and attaching a felt backing on page 13.

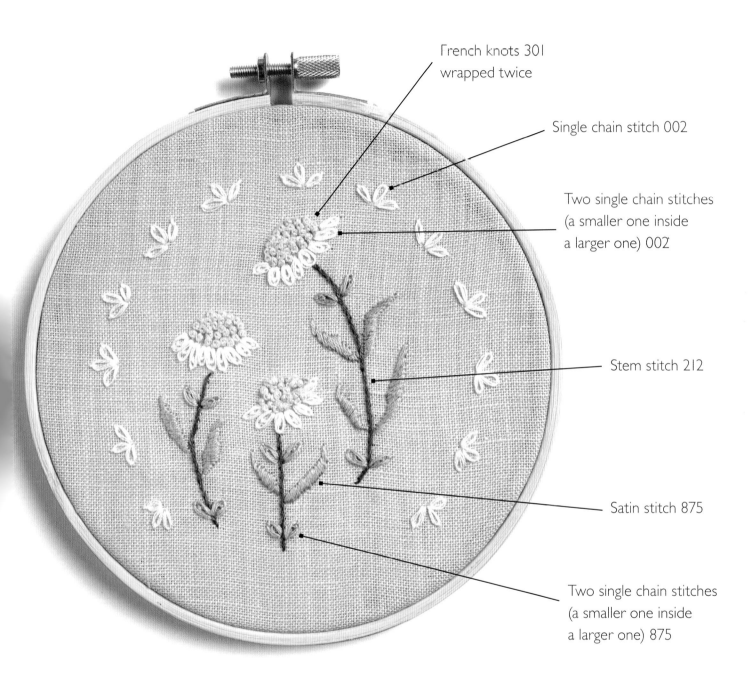

French knots 301
wrapped twice

Single chain stitch 002

Two single chain stitches
(a smaller one inside
a larger one) 002

Stem stitch 212

Satin stitch 875

Two single chain stitches
(a smaller one inside
a larger one) 875

WOOLLY SHEEP

I love how a few simple shapes placed together can create an animal with a lot of personality. I was able to mimic the texture of a woolly sheep by clustering French knots close together, and once I added the eyes, this little sheep really came to life.

SKILL LEVEL: EASY

YOU'LL NEED

FABRIC
- 8in (20cm) square blue linen fabric
- 3¾in (9.5cm) circle white felt, for backing

HOOP
- 4in (10cm) embroidery hoop

HABERDASHERY
- Thread: pearl cotton 5
    Black (Anchor 403, DMC 310)
    White (Anchor 002, DMC White)
- Thread for finishing: pearl cotton 5, White (Anchor 001, DMC White)
- Embroidery needle, size 6
- Dressmaker's carbon paper and tracing paper
- Pencil
- Scissors

Tip

This simple design uses just two shades of thread – black and white – and one stitch, the versatile French knot. Wrapping French knots three times creates dimension and texture, while the placement of the single-wrapped white eyes peeking out from the black face gives the sheep its personality.

PREPARATION

Transfer the design (see Templates, page 131) onto fabric (see page 11). Centre hoop over the design, assembling it securely (see page 12).

STITCHES USED
SEE EMBROIDERY STITCHES, PAGES 14-23

- French knot

METHOD

Using one strand of pearl cotton throughout, work the embroidery following the diagram. Wrap the French knots three times for the body, head and feet. Work the eyes last, wrapping the French knots once.

FINISHING

See instructions for gathered finish and attaching a felt backing on page 13.

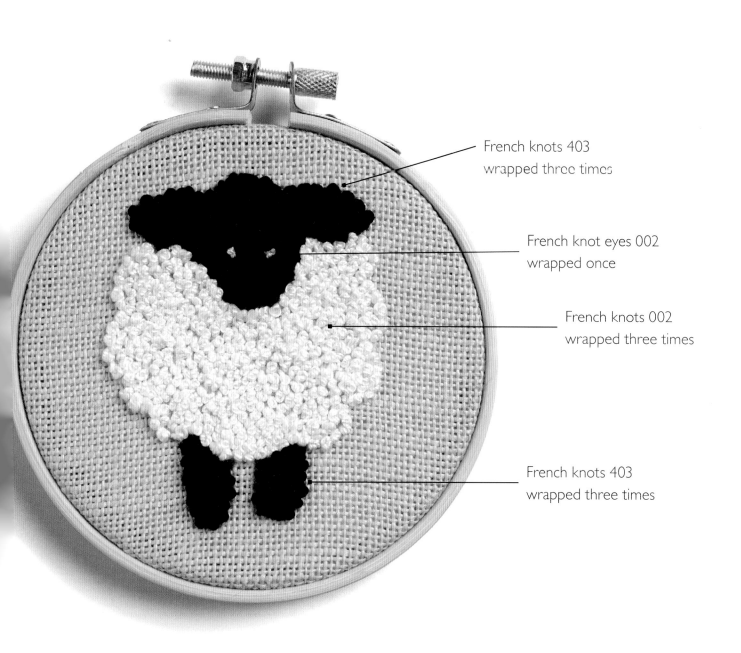

French knots 403
wrapped three times

French knot eyes 002
wrapped once

French knots 002
wrapped three times

French knots 403
wrapped three times

FLORAL SPRIG

Practise a few basic stitches to make this simple, yet sweet, flower sprig. Worked in a neutral palette, it only uses three shades of embroidery floss. You can vary it by adding colour to the petals and making the stems and leaves green.

SKILL LEVEL: EASY

YOU'LL NEED

FABRIC
- 9in (29cm) square ecru linen fabric
- 4¾in (12cm) circle white felt, for backing

HOOP
- 5in (12.7cm) embroidery hoop

HABERDASHERY
- Thread: embroidery floss
  White (Anchor 002, DMC White)
  Light Brown (Anchor 887, DMC 3046)
  Yellow (Anchor 362, DMC 437)

- Thread for finishing: pearl cotton 5,
  White (Anchor 001, DMC White)

- Embroidery needle, size 6

- Dressmaker's carbon paper and tracing paper

- Pencil

- Scissors

> **Tip**
>
> Work the flower centres by doing the satin stitch first and then adding the French knots, allowing some of the satin stitches to show through.

PREPARATION

Transfer the design (see Templates, page 130) onto fabric (see page 11). Centre hoop over the design, assembling it securely (see page 12).

STITCHES USED
SEE EMBROIDERY STITCHES, PAGES 14-23

- French knot

- Satin stitch

- Single chain stitch

- Straight stitch

- Stem stitch

METHOD

Using three strands of floss throughout, work the embroidery following the diagram. Work the stems first, then the leaves, then the petals. Add the French knots last.

FINISHING

See instructions for gathered finish and attaching a felt backing on page 13.

Single chain stitch 002

French knots 887
wrapped three times

Satin stitch 362

Stem stitch 362

Single chain
stitch 362

Satin stitch 002

Straight stitch 362

BUTTON FLOWERS

Adding buttons is a fun (and quick) way to make flower centres. I raided my button tin for an assortment of small two- and four-hole shirt and sleeve buttons for this floral array. I used a variety of solid-colour and pearlescent finishes. If you don't have a button collection yet, beware: button shopping is addictive!

SKILL LEVEL: REQUIRES SOME EXPERIENCE

YOU'LL NEED

FABRIC
- 12in (30cm) square white linen fabric
- 7¾in (19cm) circle white felt, for backing

HOOP
- 8in (20cm) embroidery hoop

HABERDASHERY
- Buttons
    3 white two-hole buttons, size ⁷⁄₁₆in (11mm)
    4 white four-hole buttons, size ⁷⁄₁₆in (11mm)
    14 white two-hole buttons, size 1¹⁄₃₂in (9mm)
    4 red two-hole buttons, size ³⁄₁₆in (6mm)
    17 red two-hole buttons, size ⅛in (5mm)
- Thread: embroidery floss
    Yellow (Anchor 291, DMC 444)
    Dark Yellow (Anchor 303, DMC 742)
    Light Orange (Anchor 314, DMC 741)
    Dark Orange (Anchor 330, DMC 947)
    Light Green (Anchor 239, DMC 702)
    Dark Green (Anchor 229, DMC 910)
- Thread for finishing: pearl cotton 5, White (Anchor 001, DMC White)
- Embroidery needle, size 6
- Dressmaker's carbon paper for tracing
- Pencil
- Scissors

> **Tip**
>
> Traditionally buttons were measured in *lignes,* from the French word for line. Today, the metric designation is more common, but if you see something like 14L on button packaging, that's why. We've provided sizes in inches and millimetres, but you can use whatever sizes, colours or finishes you like.

PREPARATION

Transfer the design (see Templates, page 132) onto fabric (see page 11). Centre hoop over the design, assembling it securely (see page 12).

STITCHES USED
SEE EMBROIDERY STITCHES, PAGES 14-23

- Stem stitch

- Satin stitch

- Straight stitch

- Fishbone stitch

- Single chain stitch

METHOD

Using three strands of floss, work all the embroidery first, following the diagram. Work the stems, the leaves, then the flowers. Sew on the buttons using three strands of floss and following the diagram for placement.

FINISHING

See instructions for gathered finish and attaching a felt backing on page 13.

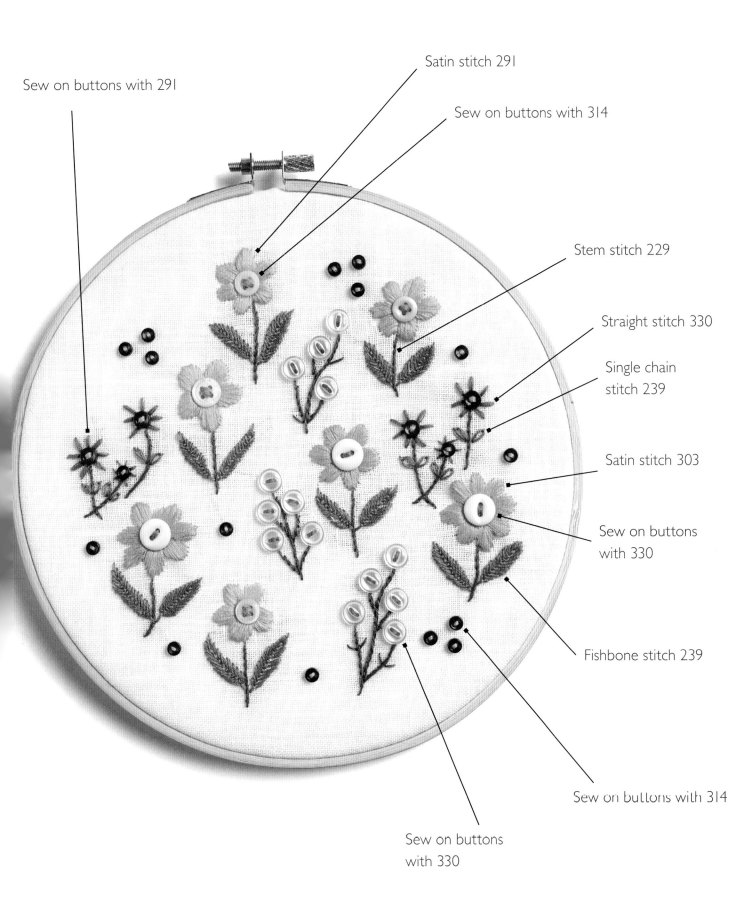

Sew on buttons with 291

Satin stitch 291

Sew on buttons with 314

Stem stitch 229

Straight stitch 330

Single chain stitch 239

Satin stitch 303

Sew on buttons with 330

Fishbone stitch 239

Sew on buttons with 314

Sew on buttons with 330

COSY JUMPER

Since I'm both a knitter and an embroiderer, designing colourwork knitting is second nature for me. But you don't have be able to knit to make this cosy jumper. I chose a classic blue and white palette – but you could try any of your favourite colour combinations, making it as simple or colourful as you want.

SKILL LEVEL: REQUIRES SOME EXPERIENCE

YOU'LL NEED

FABRIC
- 10in (25cm) blue cotton or linen square
- 5¾in (14.5cm) circle white felt, for backing

HOOP
- 6in (15.25cm) embroidery hoop

HABERDASHERY
- Thread: embroidery floss
  White (Anchor 002, DMC White)
  Light Blue (Anchor 117, DMC 341)
  Medium Blue (Anchor 131, DMC 798)
  Dark Blue (Anchor 148, DMC 311)

- Thread for finishing: pearl cotton 5, White (Anchor 001, DMC White)

- Embroidery needle, size 6

- Dressmaker's carbon paper and tracing paper

- Pencil

- Scissors

> **Tip**
>
> To mimic the look of knitting, I used satin stitch for most of the body and worked blanket stitches closely together to create the look of ribbing on the cuffs. French knots resemble knitted bobbles on the yoke. You could design your own by experimenting with stitch placement.

PREPARATION

Transfer the design (see Templates, page 133) onto fabric (see page 11). Centre hoop over the design, assembling it securely (see page 12).

STITCHES USED
SEE EMBROIDERY STITCHES, PAGES 14-23

- Outlined satin stitch

- Satin stitch

- French knot

- Blanket stitch

- Cross stitch

- Straight stitch

METHOD

Using three strands of floss throughout, work the embroidery following the diagram. First, work the medium blue satin stitch bands, then work the white and light blue satin stitch to fill in the background. Next, work the cross stitch, straight stitch and the French knots on top of the satin stitch areas.

FINISHING

See instructions for gathered finish and attaching a felt backing on page 13.

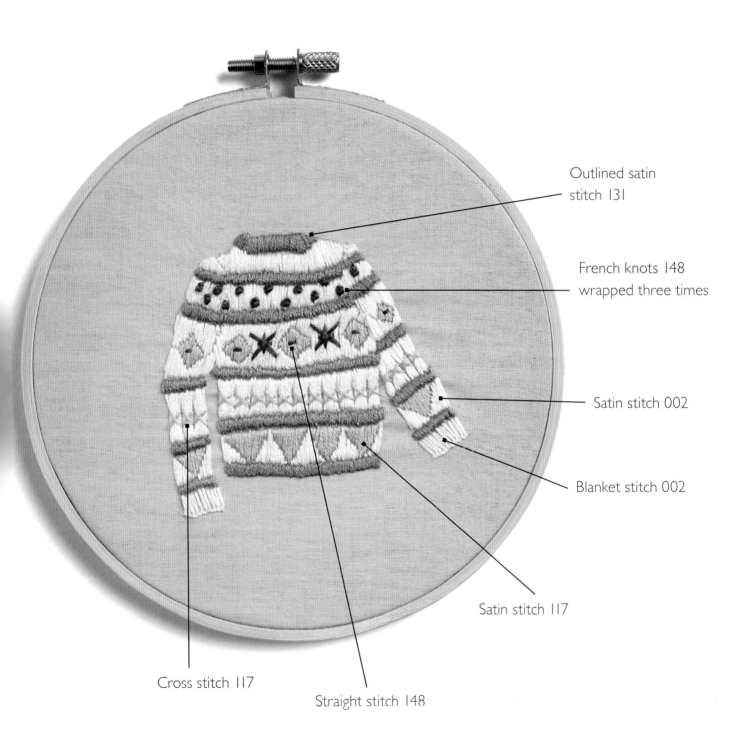

Outlined satin stitch 131

French knots 148 wrapped three times

Satin stitch 002

Blanket stitch 002

Satin stitch 117

Cross stitch 117

Straight stitch 148

SPRING GARDEN

After being deprived of fresh blooms in my garden all winter, the early spring flowers are some of my favourites. I designed this embroidery to remind me of those lovely spring days. Stitch this garden and you can have pansies, lilacs and forget-me-nots in your home all year round.

SKILL LEVEL: REQUIRES SOME EXPERIENCE

YOU'LL NEED

FABRIC

- 12in (30) square white linen fabric

- 7¾in (18cm) circle white felt, for backing

HOOP

- 8in embroidery hoop

HABERDASHERY

- Thread: embroidery floss
    Green (Anchor 241, DMC 989)
    Dark Blue (Anchor 131, DMC 798)
    Light Blue (Anchor 120, DMC 3747)
    Dark Purple (Anchor 98, DMC 553)
    Light Purple (Anchor 95, DMC 3609)
    Dark Pink (Anchor 28, DMC 956)
    Light Pink (Anchor 26, DMC 894)
    Dark Coral (Anchor 328, DMC 3341)
    Yellow (Anchor 311, DMC 3827)

> **Tip**
>
> When working with many colours, the back of your embroidery can get a little messy. To keep your work tidy, try not to carry threads of the same colour from one flower to another. Fasten off and start afresh in the next section.

- Thread for finishing: pearl cotton 5, White (Anchor 001, DMC White)

- Embroidery needle, size 6

- Dressmaker's carbon paper and tracing paper

- Pencil

- Scissors

PREPARATION

Transfer the design (see Templates, page 141) onto fabric (see page 11). Centre hoop over the design, assembling it securely (see page 12).

STITCHES USED
SEE EMBROIDERY STITCHES, PAGES 14-23

- Stem stitch

- Single chain stitch

- Straight stitch

- French knot

- Satin stitch

- Long and short stitch

METHOD

Using three strands of floss throughout, work the embroidery following the diagram. First, work the stems and leaves. Then work the single chain flowers and the small satin stitch flowers. Next, work the larger flowers. Add the French knots last.

FINISHING

See instructions for gathered finish and attaching a felt backing on page 13.

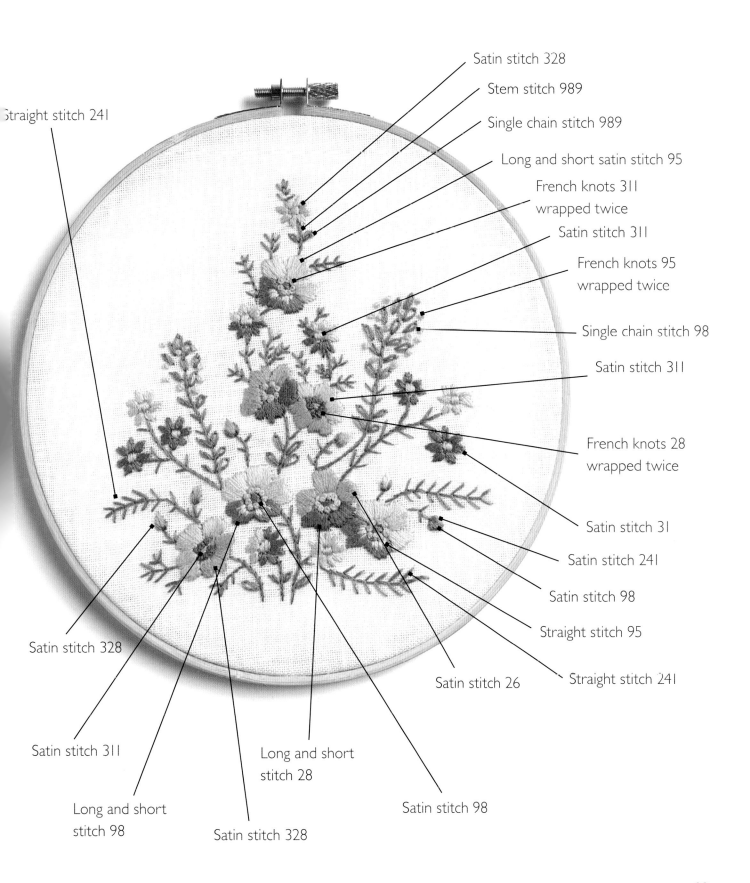

Straight stitch 241

Satin stitch 328

Stem stitch 989

Single chain stitch 989

Long and short satin stitch 95

French knots 311 wrapped twice

Satin stitch 311

French knots 95 wrapped twice

Single chain stitch 98

Satin stitch 311

French knots 28 wrapped twice

Satin stitch 31

Satin stitch 241

Satin stitch 98

Straight stitch 95

Straight stitch 241

Satin stitch 26

Satin stitch 98

Long and short stitch 28

Satin stitch 328

Satin stitch 311

Long and short stitch 98

Satin stitch 328

BLACKBERRIES

Nothing says summer like berries! I love to go berry picking and come back with baskets of them to make jam or bake pies. I designed this blackberry sprig to remind me of those midsummer excursions all year.

SKILL LEVEL: EASY

YOU'LL NEED

FABRIC
- 8in (20cm) square off-white linen
- 3¾in (7.5cm) circle white felt, for backing

HOOP
- 4in (10cm) embroidery hoop

HABERDASHERY
- Thread: embroidery floss
  Light Purple (Anchor 98, DMC 3835)
  Dark Purple (Anchor 101, DMC 550)
  Light Green (Anchor 264, DMC 334)
  Dark Green (Anchor 267, DMC 3346)

- Thread for finishing: pearl cotton 5, White (Anchor 001, DMC White)

- Embroidery needle, size 6

- Dressmaker's carbon paper and tracing paper

- Pencil

- Scissors

> **Tip**
>
> If raspberries are more your jam than blackberries, try substituting two shades of red thread for the light and dark purple. You'll have a raspberry patch instead of a blackberry bush.

PREPARATION

Transfer the design (see Templates, page 129) onto fabric (see page 11). Centre hoop over the design, assembling it securely (see page 12).

STITCHES USED
SEE EMBROIDERY STITCHES, PAGES 14-23

- Stem stitch

- Satin stitch

- French knot

- Back stitch

- Straight stitch

METHOD

Using three strands of floss throughout, work the embroidery following the diagram. First, work the stems, then the leaves. Add the French knot berries last.

FINISHING

See instructions for gathered finish and attaching a felt backing on page 13.

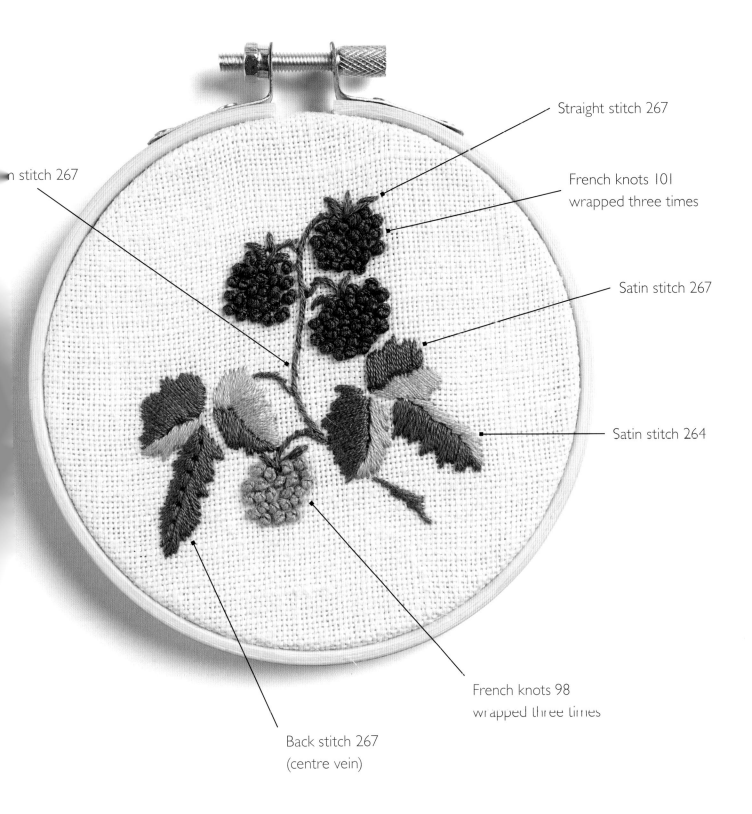

Straight stitch 267

French knots 101
wrapped three times

n stitch 267

Satin stitch 267

Satin stitch 264

French knots 98
wrapped three times

Back stitch 267
(centre vein)

CRINOLINE LADY

I get a lot of my ideas from the vintage embroidery pieces I collect. When at a boot sale or thrift shop, I always keep an eye out for pillowcases, samplers and handkerchiefs from the 1940s and 1950s, but they are getting harder to find. Stitch your own old-fashioned feminine flower girl for yourself or to give to your favourite young lady.

SKILL LEVEL: REQUIRES SOME EXPERIENCE

YOU'LL NEED

FABRIC

- 12in (30cm) square white linen fabric

- 7¾in (19cm) circle white felt, for backing

HOOP

- 8in (20cm) embroidery hoop

HABERDASHERY

- Thread: embroidery floss
    Light Pink (Anchor 50, DMC 957)
    Dark Pink (Anchor 27, DMC 893)
    Yellow (Anchor 302, DMC 743)
    Green (Anchor 241, DMC 989)
    Light Coral (Anchor 8, DMC 3824)
    Dark Coral (Anchor 9, DMC 352)
    Blue (Anchor 121, DMC 809)
    Black (Anchor 403, DMC 310)

- Thread for finishing: pearl cotton 5, White (Anchor 001, DMC White)

- Embroidery needle, size 6

- Dressmaker's carbon paper and tracing paper

- Pencil

- Scissors

> **Tip**
>
> If you are going for a vintage look, choose a soft colour palette like I've used here.

PREPARATION

Transfer the design (see Templates, page 133) onto fabric (see page 11). Centre hoop over the design, assembling it securely (see page 12).

STITCHES USED
SEE EMBROIDERY STITCHES, PAGES 14-23

- Stem stitch

- Satin stitch

- Single chain stitch

- Lazy daisy

- French knot

METHOD

Using one strand of floss for the black lines and three strands of floss for the remainder of the design, work the embroidery following the diagram. Work the lady, hat and dress first, then the flowers. Add the French knots last.

FINISHING

See instructions for gathered finish and attaching a felt backing on page 13.

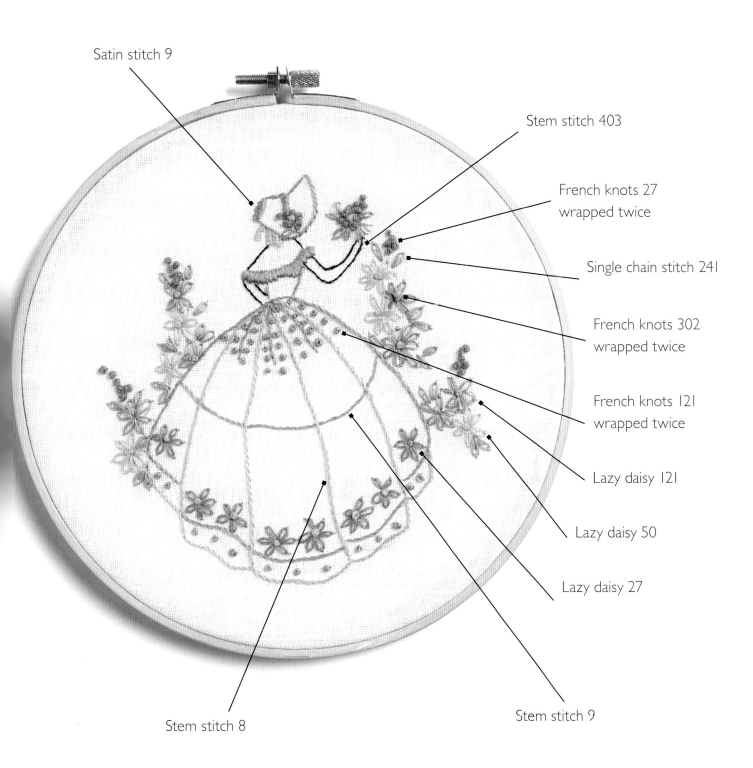

Satin stitch 9

Stem stitch 403

French knots 27
wrapped twice

Single chain stitch 241

French knots 302
wrapped twice

French knots 121
wrapped twice

Lazy daisy 121

Lazy daisy 50

Lazy daisy 27

Stem stitch 9

Stem stitch 8

VINTAGE FLOWERS

This design was inspired by a piece of vintage fabric from the 1950s that I found in my scrap basket. I chose faded pastel tones and tiny floral prints to achieve the look.

SKILL LEVEL: REQUIRES SOME EXPERIENCE

YOU'LL NEED

FABRIC

- 12in (30cm) square light blue linen or cotton fabric
- 7¾in (19cm) circle white felt, for backing
- 12 × 6in (30 × 15cm) piece of green cotton fabric (for grass)
- 1½in (4cm) diameter circle blue cotton fabric (for centre flower)
- 1½in (4cm) diameter circle pink floral fabric (cut two)
- ½in (1.5cm) diameter circle blue floral fabric (cut two)

HOOP

- 8in (20cm) embroidery hoop

HABERDASHERY

- Thread: pearl cotton 8
    White (Anchor 002, DMC White)
    Dark Green (Anchor 212, DMC 561)
    Medium Green (Anchor 208, DMC 563)
    Light Green (Anchor 264, DMC 772)
    Yellow (Anchor 301, DMC 744)
    Dark Blue (Anchor 146, DMC 798)
    Light Blue (Anchor 129, DMC 3325)
    Dark Pink (Anchor 41, DMC 893)
    Light Pink (Anchor 52, DMC 899)

- Thread for finishing: pearl cotton 5, White (Anchor 001, DMC White)

- Basting thread

- Embroidery needle, size 6

- Dressmaker's carbon paper and tracing paper

- Pencil

- Scissors

> **Tip**
>
> Try to use a tightly-woven fabric for the flowers to avoid fraying. On my sample, the embroidery stitches were enough to prevent frayed edges and the design will be staying in the hoop so I'm not worried. But if you were going to make it into a pillow or something that gets wear and tear, I'd recommend using Fray Check around the edges before you embroider.

PREPARATION

Transfer the design (see Templates, page 134) onto the fabric (see page 11). Following the template, cut out the green fabric shape for grass, leaving extra room on the bottom and sides for the hoop. Baste green fabric onto the blue background. Centre hoop over the design, assembling it securely (see page 12).

STITCHES USED

SEE EMBROIDERY STITCHES, PAGES 14-23

- Blanket stitch
- Back stitch
- Straight stitch
- Running stitch
- Fishbone stitch
- Herringbone stitch
- Single chain stitch
- Lazy daisy
- Stem stitch
- French knot

METHOD

Baste the fabric flowers onto the background fabric following the template. Using one strand of pearl cotton throughout, embroider over the fabric flowers. Work the stems and the leaves. Remove the basting threads.

FINISHING

See instructions for gathered finish and attaching a felt backing on page 13.

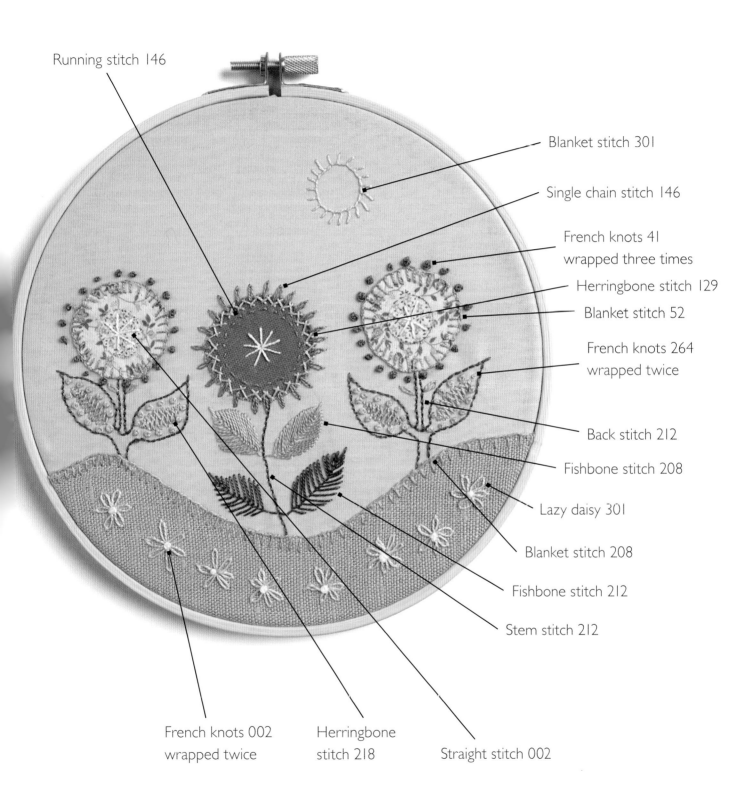

Running stitch 146

Blanket stitch 301

Single chain stitch 146

French knots 41
wrapped three times

Herringbone stitch 129

Blanket stitch 52

French knots 264
wrapped twice

Back stitch 212

Fishbone stitch 208

Lazy daisy 301

Blanket stitch 208

Fishbone stitch 212

Stem stitch 212

French knots 002
wrapped twice

Herringbone
stitch 218

Straight stitch 002

FEATHERS

I'm fascinated by birds of all kinds and their beautiful feathers. I always pick up feathers when I'm out walking and I chose these two from my collection. I love the bold colours of the blue jay and the stripes of the pheasant.

SKILL LEVEL: REQUIRES SOME EXPERIENCE

YOU'LL NEED

FABRIC

- 11in (30cm) square white linen fabric

- 6¾in (17cm) circle white felt, for backing

HOOP

- 7in (17.7cm) embroidery hoop

HABERDASHERY

- Thread: embroidery floss
  Dark Brown (Anchor 905, DMC 3021)
  Light Brown (Anchor 914, DMC 407)
  Dark Orange (Anchor 1003, DMC 921)
  Light Pink (Anchor 1011, DMC 948)
  Light Off-White (Anchor 933, DMC 543)
  Very Dark Blue (Anchor 149, DMC 803)
  Medium Blue (Anchor 147, DMC 792)
  Light Blue (Anchor 136, DMC 799)
  Very Light Blue (Anchor 144, DMC 800)

- Thread for finishing: pearl cotton 5, White (Anchor 001, DMC White)

- Embroidery needle, size 6

- Dressmaker's carbon paper and tracing paper

- Pencil

- Scissors

> *Tip*
>
> Do you have a favourite bird? Design your own feathers by changing thread colours. Love cardinals, for example? Trade red threads for the blues. This would also make a lovely gift for a bird-watching friend.

PREPARATION

Transfer the design (see Templates, page 136) onto fabric (see page 11). Centre hoop over the design, assembling it securely (see page 12).

STITCHES USED
SEE EMBROIDERY STITCHES, PAGES 14-23

- Back stitch

- Satin stitch

- Long and short stitch

- Straight stitch

METHOD

Using three strands of floss throughout, work the embroidery following the diagram. Work all the satin stitch, from light to dark. Add veins in back stitch last.

FINISHING

See instructions for gathered finish and attaching a felt backing on page 13.

Satin stitch 136

Satin stitch 144

Back stitch (spine) 933

Long and short stitch 136

Satin stitch 933

Long and short stitch 136

Satin stitch 149

Straight stitch 147

Back stitch 905

Straight stitch 914

Satin stitch 914

Satin stitch 1011

Satin stitch 905

Satin stitch 1003

HIGHLAND THISTLE

Now that you have the hang of basic embroidery stitches, it's time to delve into dimensional work. We've already used French knots to create texture. Now let's add a tassel to make a 3D thistle.

SKILL LEVEL: REQUIRES EXPERIENCE

YOU'LL NEED

FABRIC
- 8in (20cm) square white linen fabric
- 3¾in (9cm) circle white felt, for backing

HOOP
- 4in (10cm) embroidery hoop

HABERDASHERY
- Thread: embroidery floss
    Purple (Anchor 98, DMC 553) – 1 full skein for 2 tassels
    Light Green (Anchor 208, DMC 563)
    Dark Green (Anchor 210, DMC 562)

- Thread for finishing: pearl cotton 5, White (Anchor 001, DMC White)

- Embroidery needle, size 6

- Dressmaker's carbon paper and tracing paper

- Pencil

- Scissors

> **Tip**
>
> To get the dimensional effect, I first attached the tassel to the fabric at the base, close to the stem. Then I worked the stem and leaves. Next, I worked satin stitches over the bulb area, only going through the fabric at each side, which created the raised effect. (No stitches went into the tassel itself.) Lastly, I added the darker green, running it over and under the satin stitches to create the basketweave look.

PREPARATION

Transfer the design (see Templates, page 129) onto fabric (see page 11). Centre hoop over the design, assembling it securely (see page 12).

STITCHES USED

SEE EMBROIDERY STITCHES, PAGES 14-23

- Satin stitch

- Couching stitch

METHOD

Make two tassels using six strands of floss (see diagram, right). Attach to fabric following diagram (4). Work the green base of the thistle over the tassel, not through it (5).

FINISHING

See instructions for gathered finish and attaching a felt backing on page 13.

MAKING A TASSEL

1. Thread strands of floss through all the loops and make a double knot.

2. Wrap floss around the top of skein and tie securely.

3. Cut the skein above the label to make tassel.

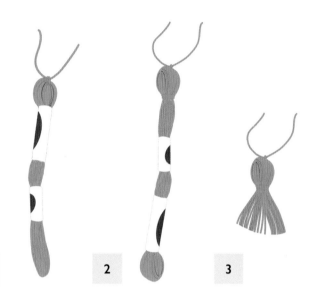

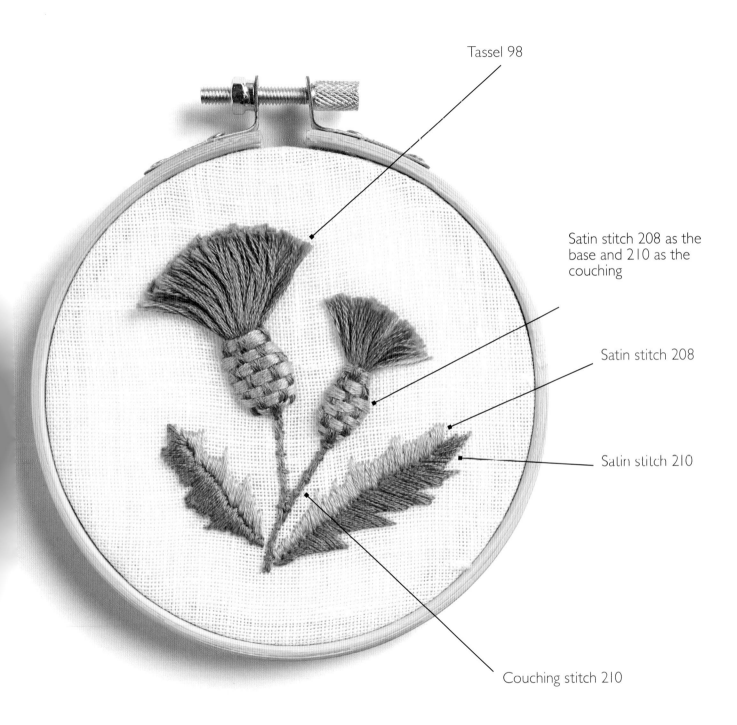

Tassel 98

Satin stitch 208 as the
base and 210 as the
couching

Satin stitch 208

Satin stitch 210

Couching stitch 210

FELT FLOWERS

You could choose any colours of felt for this bold flower garden. I love the tone-on-tone effect, but you could use multiple shades for a more boho look.

SKILL LEVEL: REQUIRES SOME EXPERIENCE

YOU'LL NEED

FABRIC

- 13in (33cm) square white linen fabric

- 8¾in (22cm) circle white felt, for backing

- For centre flower:
    2in (5cm) diameter circle medium blue felt
    1½in (4cm) diameter circle light turquoise felt
    ¾in (2cm) diameter circle medium blue felt

- For medium right flower:
    1½in (4cm) diameter circle dark turquoise felt
    ¾in (2cm) diameter circle light turquoise felt

- For medium left flower:
    1½in (4cm) diameter circle dark turquoise felt
    ¾in (2cm) diameter circle light blue felt

- For small right flower:
    1in (2.5cm) diameter circle light blue felt

- For far-left flower:
    ¾in (2cm) diameter circle dark turquoise felt

HOOP

- 9in (22.8cm) embroidery hoop

HABERDASHERY

- Thread: pearl cotton 8
    Dark Blue (Anchor 133, DMC 796)
    Dark Turquoise (Anchor 189, DMC 991)
    Light Turquoise (Anchor 847, DMC 307)
    Periwinkle Blue (Anchor 130, DMC 809)
    Dark Green (Anchor 217, DMC 367)
    Light Green (Anchor 215, DMC 320)

- Thread for finishing: pearl cotton 5, White (Anchor 001, DMC White)

- Basting thread

- Embroidery needle, size 6

- Dressmaker's carbon paper and tracing paper

- Pencil

- Scissors

Tip

I like to keep a selection of colours of felt squares on hand. Adding felt to your embroidery makes for a quick project that's fun to stitch. For this project you could easily add other elements with felt, such as a yellow sun, green leaves or even a bird or butterfly.

PREPARATION

Transfer the design (see Templates, page 135) onto fabric (see page 11). Centre hoop over the design, assembling it securely (see page 12).

STITCHES USED
SEE EMBROIDERY STITCHES, PAGES 14-23

- Blanket stitch
- Back stitch
- Fly stitch
- Straight stitch
- Herringbone stitch
- Fishbone stitch
- Satin stitch
- Single chain stitch
- French knot

METHOD

Baste the felt circles to the linen fabric following the diagram. Using one strand of pearl cotton throughout, embroider through the linen and the felt following the diagram. Then work the stems and the leaves through the linen only. Remove the basting threads.

FINISHING

See instructions for gathered finish and attaching a felt backing on page 13.

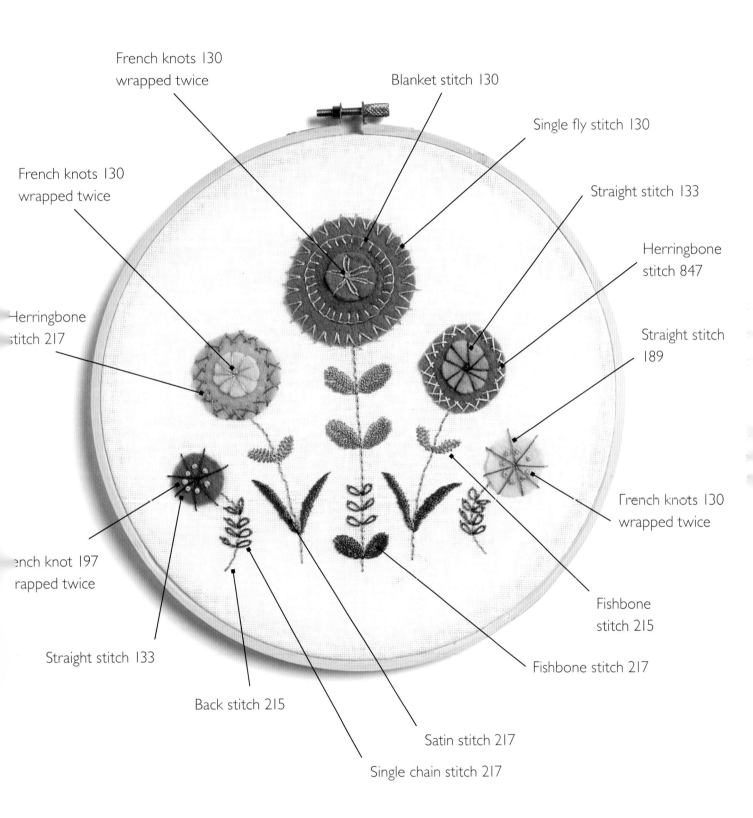

French knots 130
wrapped twice

French knots 130
wrapped twice

Blanket stitch 130

Single fly stitch 130

Straight stitch 133

Herringbone
stitch 847

Herringbone
stitch 217

Straight stitch
189

French knots 130
wrapped twice

French knot 197
wrapped twice

Fishbone
stitch 215

Straight stitch 133

Fishbone stitch 217

Back stitch 215

Satin stitch 217

Single chain stitch 217

COLOURFUL MANDALA

For my updated version of a traditional mandala – which in the Sanskrit language means 'circle' – I used felt, rather than linen fabric. The clean edges of the felt circles make it easy to work with when creating layers and give a contemporary look.

SKILL LEVEL: REQUIRES SOME EXPERIENCE

YOU'LL NEED

FABRIC
- 12in (30cm) square turquoise felt square
- 5½in (14cm) diameter white felt circle
- 3½in (9cm) diameter yellow felt circle
- 2in (5cm) diameter turquoise felt circle
- ¾in (2cm) diameter orange felt circle
- 7¾in (20cm) circle white felt, for backing

HOOP
- 8in (20cm) embroidery hoop

HABERDASHERY
- Thread: pearl cotton 5
      Orange (Anchor 332, DMC 608)
      Yellow (Anchor 288, DMC 445)
      Purple (Anchor 101, DMC 550)
      Turquoise (Anchor 188, DMC 3812)

- Thread for finishing: pearl cotton 5,
  White (Anchor 001, DMC White)

- Embroidery needle, size 6

- Dressmaker's carbon paper and tracing paper

- Pencil

- Scissors

> **Tips**
>
> To cut felt circles, first make paper templates in the required sizes. Pin each one to its coordinating felt colour. Using a pencil, draw around the circle, then cut out.
>
> Try using a bright-coloured felt for backing your mandala instead of white.

PREPARATION

Centre turquoise felt square in the hoop. Centring the felt circles, baste down white circle, then yellow, then turquoise, then orange, as shown in the image (see Templates, page 138).

STITCHES USED
SEE EMBROIDERY STITCHES, PAGES 14-23

- French knot

- Zigzag chain stitch

- Chain stitch

- Blanket stitch

- Herringbone stitch

- Straight stitch

METHOD

Using one strand of pearl cotton throughout, work the embroidery following the diagram. Remove the basting threads. Begin in the centre circle, working straight stitch to attach the orange circle. Work a herringbone stitch to attach the turquoise circle. Work buttonhole stitch to attach the yellow circle, then the white circle. Add yellow chain stitch, then orange chain stitch, then green zigzag chain stitch. Add the French knots last.

FINISHING

See instructions for gathered finish and attaching a felt backing on page 13.

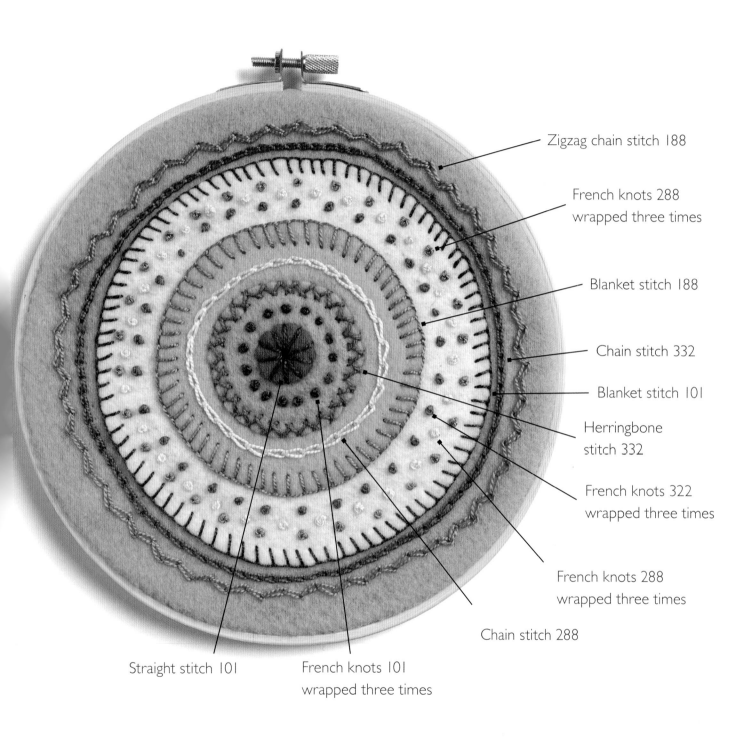

Zigzag chain stitch 188

French knots 288
wrapped three times

Blanket stitch 188

Chain stitch 332

Blanket stitch 101

Herringbone
stitch 332

French knots 322
wrapped three times

French knots 288
wrapped three times

Chain stitch 288

Straight stitch 101

French knots 101
wrapped three times

GIRL WITH A PLAIT

This charming design brings together a couple of the techniques we've learned: working with multiple stitches, adding fabric and adding dimension. I've made a thick blonde braid using six-stranded blonde-coloured floss.

SKILL LEVEL: REQUIRES EXPERIENCE

YOU'LL NEED

FABRIC

- 8in (20cm) square white linen fabric

- 8in (15cm) circle white felt, for lining

- 3¾in (9cm) circle white felt, for backing

- 2in (5cm) square blue felt, for hat

HOOP

- 4in (10cm) embroidery hoop

HABERDASHERY

- Thread: embroidery floss
  Green (Anchor 221, DMC 502)
  Yellow (Anchor 289, DMC 307)
  Dark Pink (Anchor 87, DMC 3607)
  Light Pink (Anchor 23, DMC 963)
  Blue (Anchor 131, DMC 798)
  Purple (Anchor 98, DMC 553)
  Very Light Tan (Anchor 387, DMC 739)

- Blue sewing thread (for hat)

- Thread for finishing: pearl cotton 5, White (Anchor 001, DMC White)

- Embroidery needle, size 6

- Dressmaker's carbon paper and tracing paper

- Pencil

- Scissors

> **Tip**
>
> My girl has a blue hat and a blonde plait, but yours could be a brunette, have a ponytail or two braids. Be creative with your hair styling!

PREPARATION

Transfer the design (see Templates, page 129) onto fabric (see page 11). Centre hoop over the design, assembling it securely (see page 12).

STITCHES USED
SEE EMBROIDERY STITCHES, PAGES 14-23

- Chain stitch
- Back stitch
- Single chain stitch
- Lazy daisy
- Running stitch
- French knot

METHOD

First make the plait and attach. Cut the blue felt in the shape of a hat, following the templates, and sew to the fabric with blue thread. Using three strands of floss, work the embroidery following the diagram. Work the back stitches with the number of strands listed. Do not work the French knots. Remove the embroidered piece from the hoop and centre the lining felt on top of the wrong side of the embroidery and centre it back in the hoop. (You now have two layers of fabric.) Using six strands of floss, work the French knots through both the felt lining and the linen fabric.

FINISHING

See instructions for gathered finish and attaching a felt backing on page 13.

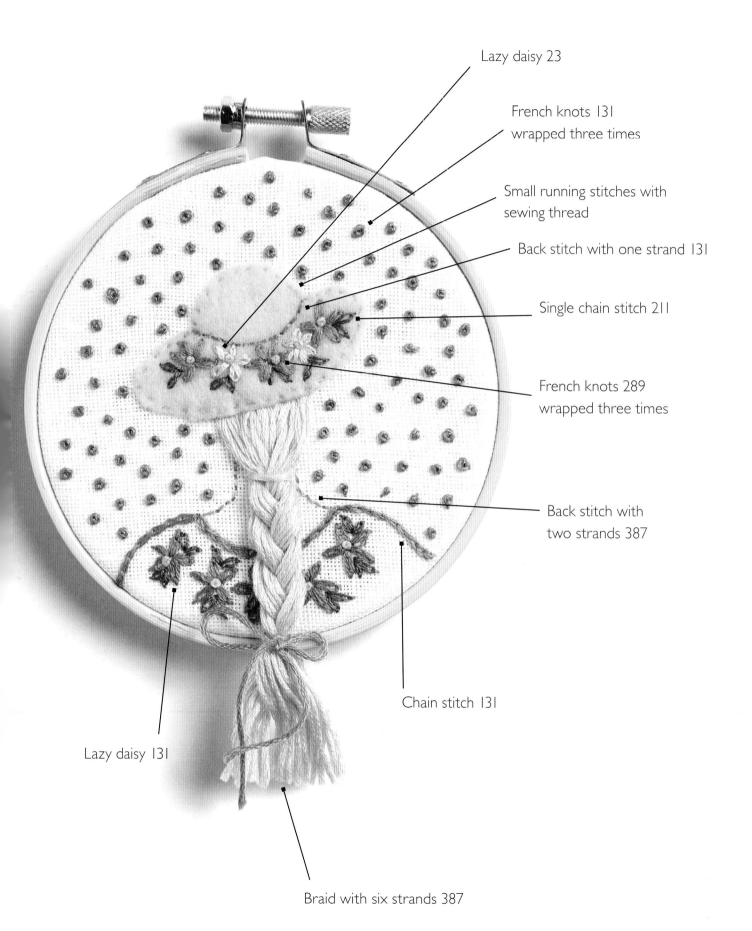

Lazy daisy 23

French knots 131
wrapped three times

Small running stitches with
sewing thread

Back stitch with one strand 131

Single chain stitch 211

French knots 289
wrapped three times

Back stitch with
two strands 387

Chain stitch 131

Lazy daisy 131

Braid with six strands 387

WINTER SNOWFLAKES

This cool wintry set would make a lovely gift or addition to your own holiday decor. I've used a pale blue ground with snow-white thread and pearl seed beads, but you could create a more dramatic effect by using a darker blue background, or go all out Christmas with red and green.

SKILL LEVEL: EASY

FOR EACH DESIGN, YOU'LL NEED

FABRIC
- 8in (20cm) square blue linen fabric
- 3¾in (10cm) circle white felt, for backing

HOOP
- 4in (10cm) embroidery hoop

HABERDASHERY
- Thread: embroidery floss
    White (Anchor 002, DMC White)

- Seed beads
    12 x 3mm pearl
    8 x 5mm pearl

- Thread for finishing: pearl cotton 5,
    White (Anchor 001, DMC White)

- Embroidery needle, size 6

- Beading needle

- Dressmaker's carbon paper and tracing paper

- Pencil

- Scissors

> **Tip**
>
> You can find seed beads in small packets at craft and hobby stores. I love adding them as a finishing touch to both simple and more complicated projects. You can experiment by substituting them in designs where French knots are called for.

PREPARATION

Transfer the design (see Templates, page 131) onto fabric (see page 11). Centre hoop over the design, assembling it securely (see page 12).

STITCHES USED
SEE EMBROIDERY STITCHES, PAGES 14-23

SNOWFLAKE 1
- Satin stitch
- Single chain stitch
- Straight stitch
- Blanket stitch

METHOD
Using three strands of floss throughout, work the embroidery following the diagram. Add the beads last.

SNOWFLAKE 2
- Chain stitch
- Fly stitch

SNOWFLAKE 3
- Chain stitch
- Straight stitch
- Back stitch
- Satin stitch

FINISHING
See instructions for gathered finish and attaching a felt backing on page 13.

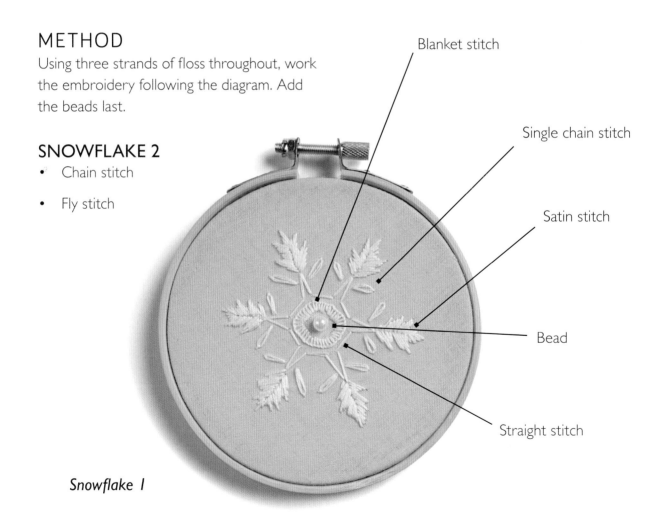

Blanket stitch

Single chain stitch

Satin stitch

Bead

Straight stitch

Snowflake 1

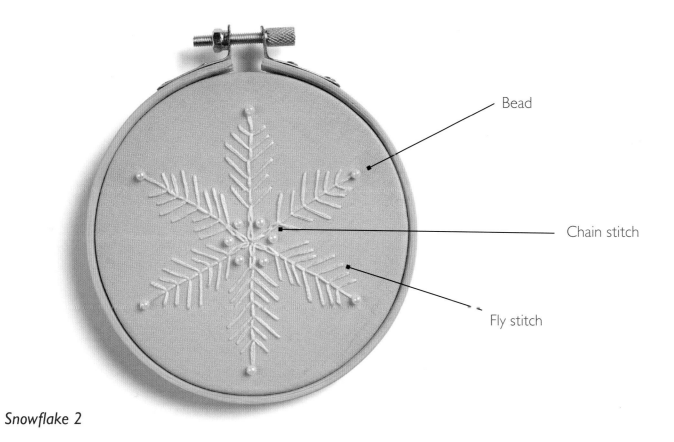

Bead

Chain stitch

Fly stitch

Snowflake 2

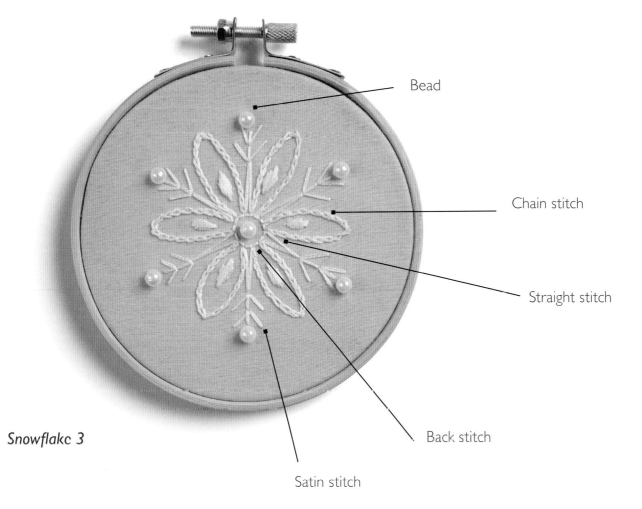

Bead

Chain stitch

Straight stitch

Back stitch

Snowflake 3

Satin stitch

BEADED HONEYBEE

Bees are essential contributors to our food supply chain: they pollinate the fruits and vegetables we eat. In this project I've used seed beads to make the characteristic yellow and black stripes of the honeybee and give it some dimension.

SKILL LEVEL: REQUIRES EXPERIENCE

YOU'LL NEED

FABRIC
- 8in (20cm) square white linen fabric
- 3¾in (9cm) circle white felt, for backing

HOOP
- 4in (10cm) embroidery hoop

HABERDASHERY
- Thread: embroidery floss
  Black (Anchor 403, DMC 310)

- Seed beads
  Yellow, approx 65 beads
  Black, approx 80 beads
  White, approx 12 beads

- Thread for finishing: pearl cotton 5, White
  (Anchor 001, DMC White)

- Embroidery needle, size 6

- Beading needle

- Dressmaker's carbon paper and tracing paper

- Pencil

- Scissors

> **Tip**
>
> If you prefer, you could swap out seed beads for French knots. Simply work rows of knots in yellow, black and white floss where I've used beads.

PREPARATION

Transfer the design (see Templates, page 129) onto fabric (see page 11). Centre hoop over the design, assembling it securely (see page 12).

STITCHES USED
SEE EMBROIDERY STITCHES, PAGES 14-23

• Back stitch

• Satin stitch

• Stem stitch

METHOD

Using one or three strands of floss throughout, work the embroidery following the diagram. Add the beads last. To attach seed beads, use a fine beading needle that will fit through the bead when threaded. (Beading needles are available in packets of assorted sizes.) Use one strand of matching floss and sew on one bead at a time. Starting at the left-hand side of the area you are beading, bring the threaded needle up from under the fabric, thread through the bead and then back through the fabric towards the right. Continue working until you have a row of beads. To secure the row you can run the needle through all of the beads, from right to left. Then begin your next row.

FINISHING

See instructions for gathered finish and attaching a felt backing on page 13.

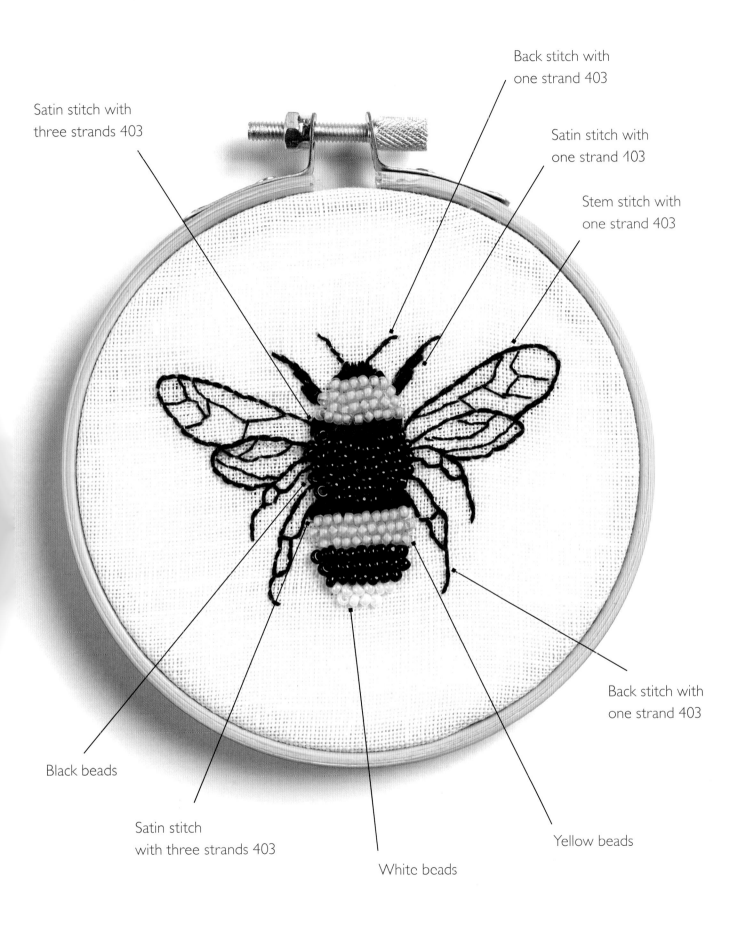

Back stitch with
one strand 403

Satin stitch with
three strands 403

Satin stitch with
one strand 103

Stem stitch with
one strand 403

Back stitch with
one strand 403

Black beads

Satin stitch
with three strands 403

Yellow beads

White beads

WOODLAND MUSHROOMS

There is something so special about finding mushrooms in the woods after a rain shower, especially the bright red fly agaric variety. They grow in circles, or 'fairy rings', and look like something out of a fairytale. Even if you haven't been lucky enough to stumble across any magical mushrooms on your walks, you can stitch some up and hope you will one day soon!

SKILL LEVEL: REQUIRES SOME EXPERIENCE

YOU'LL NEED

FABRIC
- 10in (25cm) white linen square
- 5¾in (14cm) circle white felt, for backing

HOOP
- 6in (15.25cm) embroidery hoop

HABERDASHERY
- Thread: embroidery floss
  White (Anchor 002, DMC White)
  Red (Anchor 11, DMC 350)
  Light Green (Anchor 254, DMC 472)
  Medium Green (Anchor 256, DMC 704)
  Dark Green (Anchor 258, DMC 904)
  Yellow (Anchor 293, DMC 727)
  Light Brown (Anchor 388, DMC 842)
  Medium Brown (Anchor 1082, DMC 841)

- Thread for finishing: pearl cotton 5, White (Anchor 001, DMC White)

- Embroidery needle, size 6

- Dressmaker's carbon paper and tracing paper

- Pencil

- Scissors

> **Tip**
>
> Using the red thread, outline the mushroom caps with split stich and then fill in with the satin stitches. This will give you a clean, sharp edge. Add the white French knots last, using six strands of thread to make nice chunky knots.

PREPARATION

Transfer the design (see Templates, page 137) onto fabric (see page 11). Centre hoop over the design, assembling it securely (see page 12).

STITCHES USED
SEE EMBROIDERY STITCHES, PAGES 14-23

- Outlined satin stitch

- Satin stitch

- French knot

- Blanket stitch

- Cross stitch

- Straight stitch

- Stem stitch

- Back stitch

METHOD

Using three strands of floss, work the embroidery following the diagram. Work the stalks and greenery first. Then work the flowers and gills of the mushrooms. Next work the red satin stitch to solidly fill the caps. Add the French knots on top of the red satin stitch. Note: use six strands for the white French knots and one strand for the brown French knots.

FINISHING

See instructions for gathered finish and attaching a felt backing on page 13.

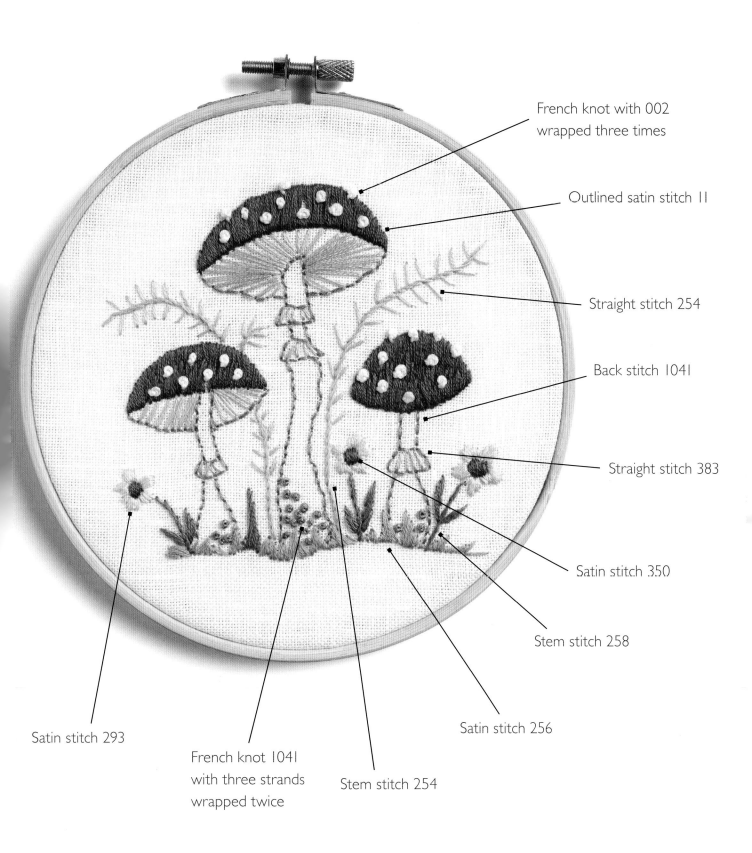

French knot with 002
wrapped three times

Outlined satin stitch 11

Straight stitch 254

Back stitch 1041

Straight stitch 383

Satin stitch 350

Stem stitch 258

Satin stitch 256

Satin stitch 293

French knot 1041
with three strands
wrapped twice

Stem stitch 254

TEMPLATES

Over the following pages are the templates required for the projects. All templates are 100% unless otherwise stated.

BICYCLE & BALLOONS (PAGE 56)

BEADED HONEYBEE (PAGE 120)

HIGHLAND THISTLE (PAGE 100)

BLACKBERRIES (PAGE 84)

GIRL WITH A PLAIT (PAGE 112)

FLORAL SPRIG (PAGE 68)

CAT IN THE WINDOW (PAGE 30)

SEASHELLS (PAGE 34)

WINTER SNOWFLAKES (PAGE 116)

WOOLLY SHEEP (PAGE 64)

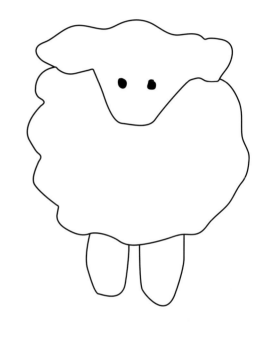

BERRY WREATH (PAGE 48)

BUTTON FLOWERS (PAGE 72)

COSY JUMPER (PAGE 76)

CRINOLINE LADY (PAGE 88)

FELT FLOWERS (PAGE 104)

HANGING BASKETS (PAGE 38)

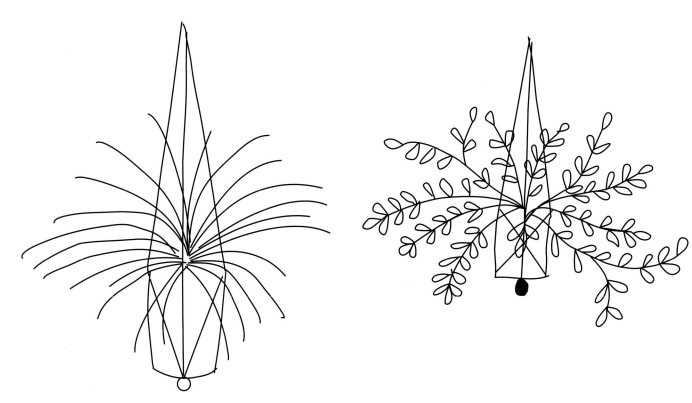

FEATHERS (PAGE 96)

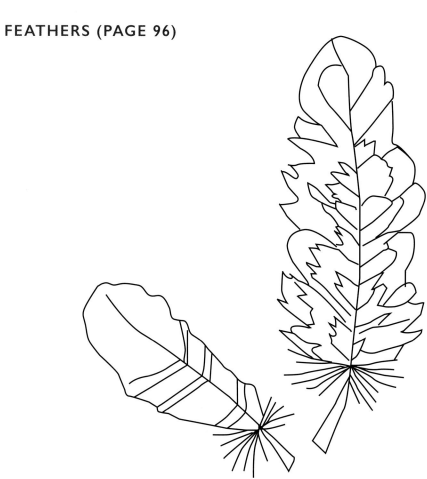

WOODLAND MUSHROOMS (PAGE 124)

FANTASY FLORALS (PAGE 44)

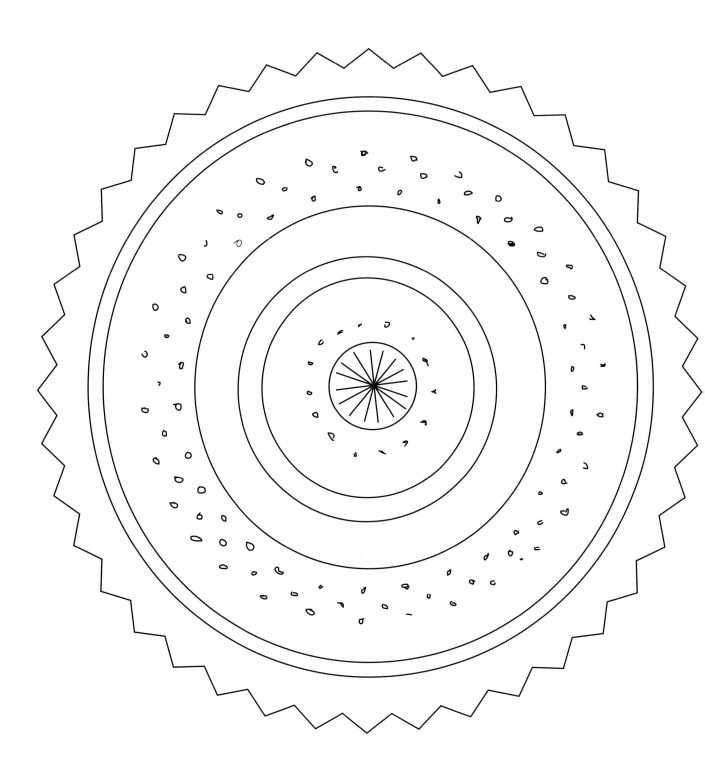

MEADOW CLOVER (PAGE 52)

WHIMSICAL DAISIES (PAGE 60)

RESOURCES

Fabric, felt, thread and embroidery hoops:
Amazon – amazon.co.uk
Hobbycraft – hobbycraft.co.uk

Embroidery floss and pearl cotton:
Anchor – anchorcrafts.com
DMC – dmc.com

ACKNOWLEDGEMENTS

I would like to thank the talented staff at Quail Studio for creating such a beautiful book. Special thanks to my friend, Trisha Malcolm, for encouraging me to pick up my embroidery needle again, and thanks to my editor, Karin Strom. I could not have created the embroideries without the support of my family and friends who spurred me on during the good days and through these challenging times. Lastly, I owe all this to a wonderful lady, Joan Toggitt, who guided me on my long and wonderful career in the embroidery world, even long after she had left us.
She was, and still is, my guardian angel.

INDEX

To order a book, or to request
a catalogue, contact:

GMC Publications Ltd
Castle Place, 166 High Street,
Lewes, East Sussex,
BN7 1XU
United Kingdom
Tel: +44 (0)1273 488005
www.gmcbooks.com